Wayward

Fetching Tales from a Year on the Road

by

Tom Gates

Wayward One Press

Beverly Hills, CA 90212

Wayward

Tom Gates © 2012

Published by: Wayward One Press, Beverly Hillls, CA 90212

Cover Art Design: Sam Means

Interior Book Design by: Booknook.biz

Contents:

New York
betsy from columbus, run down by a bus   9
my first date with matt gross, the frugal traveler   11
patti smith and my last night as a new yorker   15

Chile
notes on how not to write a book   19
on drowning   23

Argentina
as filthy as a gay man on a saturday night   29
obama day   33

Fiji
yaqueta island, fiji   37

Bali
coming up in ubud and down in kuta   43

Singapore
singapore and the gum thing   45

Malaysia
cameron highlands, malaysia   47

Vietnam

notes from vietnam   51
the underdog   55
homestayin'   59

Laos

from a flashpacker to a backpacker   63

India

it could have been a tuesday night in connecticut,
except i was on a river in india   67

England

locked down at heathrow   71

Germany

are you getting it? really getting it?   77
woe was me   81

Italy

florence defaced by graffiti, declared ugly and depressing   89

France

star trek in french, as told by
somebody who doesn't speak french   91
whilst traveling via eurail   95
the best hostel in france (is going off tonight)   99

California

notes from the grand del mar hotel, san diego   103
the patron saint of my round-the-world trip   109
notes from a round-the-world comedown   115

please note   119
about the author   121

Wayward

Fetching Tales from a Year on the Road

W hat follows is a collection of pieces largely written during a yearlong trip around the world. Several have been published and some are simply heart-felt and deranged ramblings best kept to myself, because nobody should ever read them.

Oh, shit.

betsy from columbus, run down by a bus

I think it's the walking that is doing me in. Taking me beyond the normal New Yorker stress. Getting me close to going Pacino With A Gun.

It's not just the tourists, eyes perpetually pointed skyward at the pretty buildings, aiming their bodies towards my blazing, efficient path. These folks are merely the impala of my urban animal kingdom; cheap eats for oncoming trucks, for eight-inch curbs.

It's fun to watch Betsy from Columbus, proudly displaying her minus-ten body fresh from a summer program at Curves, trouncing blindly into a Don't Walk. We New Yorkers know to weave down another avenue, because soon it will be all crowds and sirens. And police reports.

This kind of foot traffic is du jour for me, easily elbowed and knocked aside. Lately though, it's the iPhone people who are making my blood boil. New York, a town of born walkers, is crazy with pedestrians looking at their hands, typing messages into one device or another. It's Luddites Gone Wild.

Basic motor skills (look where you're going) have been lost on a Darwinian scale, bred out in just one generation. Everywhere tech-seduced tourists are headed straight into the path of businessmen, fingers blistering urgent messages. "WAS, did we jst brk up?"

On top of this, there is now The Hawker Thing. The streets are filled with pay-by-the-hour workers, trying to sell ridiculous concepts like Cranberry Yogurt and votes for John McCain.

Most lead with a forced-smile line, one that that screams for pity. "Do you have a minute for World Peace?" Four more blocks, "Do you like stand-up comedy?" Two more, "Have you tried Domino's new oven baked sandwiches?" The messages blend together and by the time I've reached home, I don't know whether to adopt a child or eat a Pop Tart.

Take this image of our streets and now factor in cabbies from Grand Theft Auto School. Toss in a few bike messengers rushing orders for big tips. Add daytime drunks, ditzy broads, joggers and assholes like me. It's getting ugly.

It's shocking for me to discuss my growing loath for the bustle of Manhattan, a place that I used to praise like a zealot. But lately – and maybe finally – it's just become too much. Guliani swept the dirt under the rug and somehow allowed in a bit too much sunshine.

Now all I can see are the parts where the molding doesn't quite meet the door frame. I find myself actually wondering if Paul Theroux might be right, if New York has become an example of what he dislikes about cities, places that are "vertiginous, threatening, monochromatic, isolating, exhausting, germ-laden, bristling with busy shadows and ambiguous odors."

All of this business with the people walking into one another – it somehow makes the sirens seem louder, the garbage trucks arrive earlier in the morning and the homeless more zombie-like. It makes me want to put on my iPod and not interact. To shut my windows and make love to Tivo. The City That Never Sleeps is beginning to make me a shut-in and it's scaring the living hell out of me.

If there was one thing I was certain of it was that New York City was my home, that I was of a breed that is impervious to all of this commotion. I think maybe that this city now belongs to a new model, a 2.0 that I don't want to become.

New York City, quite possibly, does not compute any longer.

my first date with matt gross, the frugal traveler

I had never been to a bookstore reading before tonight. My distaste has had nothing to do with the author, who is often simply whored out on a press junket, kneeling in front of the genitals of potential amazon.com five-star reviewers. I can swallow that concept just as fast as the author can swallow the ejaculation that comes in the form of praise. Rather, my apathy seems more rooted in a suspicion that the audience would be a congregation of fucking dweebs.

Tonight's little thingy at Idlewild Books didn't completely upend this philosophy but it did help me turn a corner towards coming to terms with my own little inner dork.

I should start by saying that Idlewild Books in New York City is to a travel writer what Al's House Of Titty Porn is to a porn addict. Mecca. Devoted entirely to travel, each section is arranged by location, as is custom. The owners have gone to great pains to include reading beyond guidebooks for each territory, therefore allowing for a piddly brain like mine to understand the cultural magnitude of places that my public-schooled-ass might not have known.

Borges' *Collected Fictions* and Bruce Chatwin's *In Patagonia* sit right next to *Moon Buenos Aires* and *Lonely Planet Argentina*. All of this is housed in a loft that feels decorated by real people and not architects who love to frolic in plywood. It felt like I was in San Francisco instead of New York City. That's a huge deal in Manhattan.

The reason for tonight's gathering of thirty-odd people was a talk by Matt Gross, otherwise known as The Frugal Traveler from *The New York Times*. Something of a Menudo scenario, Matt inherited the column from several other writers who have come in and out of the section since 1994. He's added a blog topspin that seems to have breathed new life into the section.

It must be a sensational burden to begin your day with a word as un-sexy as "frugal" stamped on your byline. The thing is, Matt Gross is kind of a piece of ass. He's got the geekchic thing nailed and could easily be a member of Weezer or Modest Mouse. He rocked a fresh new traveler beard, an early 90's Gap sensibility and an endearing sense of humility. He was obviously well traveled and mentioned the name of each country with perfect pronunciation ("Oor-O-Gway"), yet pulled it off without a sense of self-importance. He ended up being sweet and disarming from the get-go, almost suspiciously so. I'm not suggesting anything terribly nefarious, but he might be the kind of guy who secretly harbors anal beads in the way-back of his closet.

Over the course of thirty minutes he read passages from a few books (lamenting the recent suicide of David Foster Wallace in one reading) and told a few tales from his recent Grand Tour of Europe, during which he re-imagined the "classic European journey" on less then 100 Euros a day. He covered everything from solo-traveler-psychology to Cambodian brothels to Organic Apple Farms to The French Riviera to the benefits of a Capitol One Visa card. There was no annoying reach for an overall theme or continuity, which went perfectly well for my ADD-riddled mind. I fucking loved the guy.

I have to admit the crowd was not as bad as I had imagined. Sure, there were the people who hung on every word and guffawed at even the weak jokes. There were the wine-grabbers, a couple of mid-thirties women who downed thirteen (counted) glasses of free wine between them. Or the lady who farted. Or the man who repeatedly licked the ghost of cheese from his fingers. Overall though, this was a group of people that I would probably like to hang out with. In fact, they might be the exact crew that I would choose if I could cherry-pick the other passengers of a hellish, six hour chickenbus ride through Peru.

Frugal Matt says that he's been working on a book, tentatively titled *Just Go*. It seems to be an inspirational kick-in-the-ass for mainstreamers who might be wary of trying new places and new things.

I left Matt and Idlewild with my travel itch in high gear, knowing that there was an adventure around the corner in my life. The whole night gave me a kick in the pants to get going with my trip, to be done with the numbing day job and really try something crazy. Like write my way around the world.

So thanks, Matt. Maybe I'll just go.

patti smith and my last night as a new yorker

I promoted Patti Smith's albums from 1996 to 1998. I first met her while she was living in Detroit, shortly after the death of her husband Fred. She was just starting to poke her head up again as a full-time performer, not having released an album since 1988, a year during which I was still purchasing records from RATT. Expecting a simple record signing, I watched in amazement as hundreds of fans lined up for autographs and showered her with stories. I watched in equal shock as she drove up for the next day's concert at Pine Knob Amphitheater, her band members and gear scrunched into a compact car that wasn't fit to hold the contents of a dorm room, let alone the gear of a landmark group of rock pioneers.

It used to drive (then Arista label president) Clive Davis crazy that Patti wasn't on mainstream radio or MTV. He'd slap me around for answers, because I was the poor soul who was supposed to get her music played alongside of Limp Bizkit. The biggest jewel in his Rock Crown, she was one of the few rock artists he had worked with that would engage him on a Whitney Houston Level, accepting his advice or encouragement. He liked to drop names like Springsteen and Dylan but I never got the feeling that those guys gave him the time of day, beyond a photo op and a signature on their royalty checks. Patti actually engaged him, even lauded him.

She was a bargaining chip he'd drop at every meeting with unsigned artists. "I've always let Patti Smith be the artist that she wants to be."

Once snagged in his net, he'd tell the same artists to re-mix their singles, re-arrange their artwork and "ask" them to work with co-writers.

Not Patti. He would do anything to keep her, and to keep her happy. This is not to insinuate that she was just a bargaining chip for Clive – he would become incredibly alive when talking about her music, in a way that I didn't always hear him talk about other artists on the label. Of course, these artists were Ace Of Base and Kenny G.

Patti was never under the illusion that she was going to get her music played next to Celine Dion or Bone Thuggs-N-Harmony. She didn't have a manager and would call to check in herself. "Tom, how's the song goin'? Are people playin' it?" She always spoke in n's and didja's – she was never inclined to take the Madonna Speech Therapy Class. To a person who did not know her, they'd probably think that she worked in hardware store. Anyone who has spent time with her, though, will verify that she's more astute and learned than most people with a doctorate. And not even close to a show-off about it.

"Patti on line one." I had gotten somewhat used to the fact that she was calling me. She knew I was half her age, she knew I had my work cut out for me and she, above all, probably knew that I was the kind of guy who would not survive corporate culture. It wouldn't have surprised her if I admitted that I'd have diarrhea on the days where I'd have meeting with the Senior Vice Presidents in my nice clothes. My shelf life was obvious to everyone – even I was surprised that I had lasted four years.

One day I fucked up. I had arranged for heritage rock station WXRT to record Patti's show in Chicago – I'd venture to say that this recording might be the best live album never released, a double-disc of an artist and her band at their comeback prime. But recording this show had meant signatures, budgets and putting my ass on the line. I became so consumed with the politics that I had forgotten to tell one person the show was being recorded. Patti Smith.

She called me from the venue. "Why are there recording trucks here?" I realized, yes, I was that fucking stupid. I coughed up the truth and braced myself, the way a kid does when he has to tell a parent that he peed his pants at nine years old. I could hear her processing, taking a deep breath. "Do you understand why this makes me upset?" Then, for about ten minutes, she explained why it was important for me to have told her about this and what we could have done better if I had. I had expected the back of her hand and I was given a mom's lesson instead.

It wouldn't be the last time that I'd get a sit-down and it's safe to say that I've learned almost everything about how an artist works from Patti Smith. Often by just being present when she was around.

For example, she always focused on the person she was talking to, even if it was half-in-the-bag fan gassing about a show in 1974. You meet few artists who can do this with any sort of sincerity, especially after they come offstage, high on adrenaline. Most hide - I don't blame them. I wouldn't know how to deal.

One particular time we were backstage at Lincoln Center, after she had just given a keynote speech during a convention for college students. We were talking about how it went when a loud blond elbowed her way into our conversation. "Just one second please", Patti offered politely, sternly. She then turned her attention back to me, finishing the conversation. It didn't matter that the loud blond was Courtney Love – she just wanted to finish who she was talking to. Diarrhea Boy.

Patti's fans are devout and often romanticize her impact on the world, building her up to be some sort of faith healer. They definitely remember the moment that they first heard her, they certainly remember the first time they saw her live and they always tell the story about both. Many bear resemblance to the educators at Hogwarts School Of Witchcraft and Wizardry, a rag-tag group of post-punkers who have now gone grey and are no longer holding the mayo. They turn out in full force when she plays.

It seemed right that my last night as a New Yorker was Patti's gig at Bowery Ballroom. The show is an annual event that happens on her birthday and feels like a coming-together for all of those folks who really used to go to Max's Kansas City, who really used to paint at Chelsea Hotel and really screwed their way through the seventies.

At 61, Patti still puts on a hell of a gig. I found myself hanging in the back, smiling at the joy and enthusiasm of the witches and warlocks. I grinned as she spat on the stage between verses and as she let herself get caught up in the energy of her still-powerful band. I left before the end of the show, completely exhausted from packing up everything that I owned. I had seen what I needed to see and heard what I needed to hear.

A woman stopped me as I was walking out. "What's the matta? You not diggin' Patti?"

Oh yeah. I'm digging her.

notes on how not to write a book

My bags were greeted at Santiago's airport by two adorable drug dogs. They had taken to treating the carousel like a ride at Disneyworld, sitting on the conveyor belt for minutes at a time, pretending to sniff bags but really just slacking off.

I knew where the dogs were coming from, having spent the past year ambling through my new York City life without much care, and without a goal. I went to Chile with purpose, knowing that this was the moment I would really have to start writing a book. Little notebooks would have to be purchased, little notes would have to be inserted into them and little me would have to make sense of it all.

With this in mind, I did exactly what all writers do. I came up with distractions to put the process off even longer.

The first came in the form of a physiotherapist from The Netherlands, whom I'd met at my hostel. Michael was a man so in shape that I couldn't even be attracted to him, knowing that if we pressed our bodies together I would inexplicably combust.

He told me over a traditional Chilean meal of beans n' something why he was traveling. He had gotten into his career because he wanted to help people, realizing too late that his job would really consist of covering doctor's asses against malpractice suits and filing paperwork. He was taking some time off and trying to figure out how to actually help people, with the possibility of somehow working with war veterans. He threw it my way in plain clothes. "I am too young for this bullshit."

The next day I met up with Robert, a photographer originally from Washington DC, who had started an entertainment-based English website here in Santiago.

Robert, like me, had become disillusioned with his job in America, which had something to do with Economics. He moved to Santiago and began taking pictures, mostly of student protests. His head was quickly split open by a rock, an event he talks about the way some people talk about a delicious lasagna.

Cathy, a fellow travel writer, asked me to consume large quantities of beer and french fries with her the next day. We got to talking about Chileans, and South Americans in general. I brought up how unbelievably attached the couples around town had seemed, hanging from each other and gnashing faces, only seconds after exhaling a shared Marlboro Light. She explained that being attached is en vogue, en masse. In Santiago, being mounted by a lover in public is a lot like showing off new sneakers or a Beemer.

The more make-outty you can be, the better for your reputation. That's why people hang out drinking beer until all hours, devouring Someone Special on the white plastic chairs that always adorn the curbs of the bars here.

I cautiously suggested that women seemed to suck face with a bit of buyer's remorse, some actually gazing at me while kissing their passionate boyfriends. She confirmed that I was not imagining this, explaining that it seems as if the women adorn the men out of some sort of duty. A woman may have somewhere better to be but it is her job as girlfriend to make a spectacle of their relationship.

Another item on my list of confusing customs: Never have I seen mothers fawn over their children so much. It hasn't been uncommon to see a mother kiss her son ten times in five minutes, even if he is fourteen and wants no part of a MILF PDA.

Once I noticed this trait, I began to recognize that it was sort of creepy. The mothers seemed obsessed with their children's every move. Touching them, kissing them, holding them. My philosophy became that the mothers, who seldom seemed to have a husband in tow, have transferred the appalling affection that their husbands formerly gave them, before the zing went out of the thing. Children filled the void, allowing for endless adoration. Until puberty when, like I said, the whole thing just gets weird.

Cathy's take was also interesting. She felt Americans put too much emphasis on "one moment" for affection (a birthday, a goodnight kiss), making that one moment mean everything in the world. The South Americans, she suggested, have completely flipped this premise, choosing a quantitative approach to showing their love.

I headed back to my dorm room, looking for more distractions. The only other inhabitant was a woman who would not stop talking, not even for a second. She was about thirty and unable to be in a room with others unless she was chatting, yammering, expounding or cooing. When others spoke, her eyes grew into saucers of interest, her breath held for the moment that she could pounce into the conversation with trivia about tree sap, Bolivia or meningitis.

Within minutes I was looking for any escape from her conversation flytrap, trying desperately to think of something –anything – that could be important enough to take me away from this lady. It turns out I had the perfect excuse. I started writing the damned book.

on drowning

I used to manage a band called The Format. They ceased to exist one year ago today.

I was in Bali, about four weeks into a break that coincided with the band's writing period (those gaps between records are actually used for developing relationships, writing about them, then fucking them up by leaving for 16 months). The band's principle songwriters, Nate and Sam, had a method for writing that was frustrating enough to send me packing. For example:

Me: So where are you at with new songs?
Nate: We'll be ready.
Me: It's cute that you would think I'm that dumb. Where are you at with the songs?
Nate: We have some stuff.
Me: Songs or parts of songs?
(pause)
Nate: We know how all of the parts are going to go together. So, songs.
Me: But they're not songs yet.
Nate: They're parts of songs that form songs.
Me: I understand.
(pause)
Me: So, when are you writing the songs?
(pause)
Nate: We were talking about it while playing Halo last night.

Me: Oh, that's a relief to hear. At least you're getting together and talking about it.

Nate: Oh, no. Sam was at his house and I was at mine. We were on headsets during the game.

Me: You're writing songs with a video game as the conduit?

Nate: Chill out. You're starting to sound like an old person.

The day in question had already been one of the worst I'd had in years. I had found a boy floating facedown in the hotel pool, pulling him out with another guest and watching as a hapless lifeguard attempted to bring him back to life. I went back to my room after the coroner finally arrived, his mother making noises like those of a person trying to breathe shortly before a fifth round of water boarding. I trembled on the turquoise couch in my air-conditioned room, then found my phone and checked messages, glad for any distraction that they could provide.

A voicemail from Sam. "Dude, you should call me."

I've heard parents talk about the nuances of their babies' noises and about how they know exactly what each sound means, even if the child has not yet learned to speak. A musician's manager will also tell you that they can hear these tones from the artists with whom they work, and that "call me" voicemails can go unreturned for at least a few hours if necessary. "*You should call me*" is very different. It often means that the band's recording session is a complete disaster, that the artist wants to pull off of a tour or that the van's rear axle has inexplicably fallen onto the ground. These calls always involve strife, dismay and some kind of cop/caper bailout plan. I was quite sure that Sam would tell me that we were going to push back the making of their third album, which would mangle several months worth of scheduling and preparation. It was an annoyance but an annoyance that I was paid for, nonetheless.

"You're gonna hate me," said Sam. I knew it – we were pushing back recording. "Um, no dude. You should sit down." He would explain to me over the course of the next hour that the band was taking a hiatus, "or something."

I wasn't prepared for this. I asked hundreds of questions, in an attempt to figure out what might be done to put this back together. A manager looks to fix things, because most Total Fucking Freakouts (TFF's) last exactly 24-36 hours and number 7-10 per year. Yet, as the minutes went by, the conversation felt more like someone soft-selling a breakup (Sam) in an attempt not to hurt the other party (me). He kept trying to make it not sound like a big deal because he knew that aside from all of the things this would do to the band members, it was also going to ruin me. I'd spent the previous two years helping to rebuild The Format's career, betting that their future success would justify the extraordinary amount of time that managing their scenario entailed. Their breakup was the equivalent of folding my cards with four aces.

To review. The rejuvenation of The Format's career was a hot story, mostly because the odds were completely against it happening at all. It was an anomaly that had come with hard work, screwball determination and a total turn of luck. I had begun managing them at the end of their first album's cycle, a moment during which any person with common sense would have run quickly, just to get away from the sinkhole that regularly appeared at their feet. Still, based on recommendations from a few trusted friends and some incredible new demos, I flew to Phoenix to meet with them.

Nate and Sam picked me up in their touring van, sticking me in the back with a roped-down Wurlitzer and mismatched guitar amps. I found this wildly charming, although I might have pretended to be inconvenienced at the time. Over the next few hours we would discuss everything that had happened to them thus far. Signed amidst huge buzz, then just 18. Making an album under the thumb of a major label, with multiple producers and huge sums of money spent. The same record label being bought just after the band's album was released, practically assuring that it would get lost in the shuffle of commerce. An ungodly amount of touring. A slow and steady rise in audience, despite indifference from radio stations and magazines. And through it all, just enough money to get them through to the next tour and keep them from giving up.

The story amounted to these two kids bashing their heads against a wall for three years, knowing that they had something worthwhile but unable to find strong support, beyond their booking agent and lawyer (it should be noted here that the band's new label had some solid supporters but were caught in an industry quagmire, what with eleven year old kids becoming able to get music for free - for eternity - on their six hundred dollar computers). On the surface, especially to the music biz, the album was a complete flop.

Sitting in front of me were two young men who were nothing short of desperate. They both smoked an extraordinary amount of cigarettes, perhaps one for every minute in an hour. Their knees shook through the holes in their jeans and they both picked at their food in a way that suggested apathy for the thing that might keep them alive for the next day. It wasn't sadness or despondency; it was pure depression.

We agreed to work together and they were dropped from their label within a few months.

For the next couple of years, these two guys would work nonstop, doing almost anything that I asked them to do. The bad examples are hilarious and, given my ego, must appear in their stories and not mine. We opted to release their second record with only the help of the company that I worked for, a concept that is now gaining popularity but seemed like assisted suicide at the time. We tricked out the internet, trying almost anything that was invented in any given week, with the band's newfound freedom allowing us to out-maneuver the sluggish beasts that are known as Major Record Labels (not without making some major errors in judgment along the way). Nate answered the same ten questions about 5,000 times, in twenty languages. Sam minded to the business, phoning daily to keep tabs on finances and projections.

In short, we kicked some serious ass and created our own luck using the technology that confused most other contemporary recording artists.

We kept everything together with duct tape and crazy glue, selling about 70,000 albums over the first twelve months. The band shouldered all of the marketing costs but ultimately saw a lion's share of the revenue. We threw in one last tour before the end of the album's cycle, deciding to give away the album for free on its one year anniversary. *Dog Problems* was downloaded by 30,000 people that week and the tour sold out as fast as the link went around. We were learning that one empty pocket might somehow line the other with a fistful of bills. A show at The Mayan Theatre was recorded and released on DVD. It documented a band that was about to have it all, on their own terms and after the industry had left them for dead.

Which brings me to Bali, to the boy dying and to the "or something" that had befallen The Format.

As strange as it may seem, I do not think of the boy in the pool very often. He seems faint to me, a person whom shaped my life but only in a way that would come out in a wallet-breaking shrink session. I'd bet that both his mother and I have figured out the same thing in the past year: We are not in control. We, the people who can shape and steer, do not hold the power. The control belongs to the boy and, possibly, his creator. We will never learn why he drowned, what we could have done better or if we might have saved him. We did the best that we could, we made the best choices possible and we'll live with the consequences, for better or for worse.

So, here I am, one year later, on a rooftop in Chile.

Sam is creating music as a soundtrack-maker and is also whispering about a new project. He's started a merchandise company built on integrity and heart, which makes perfect sense if you know Sam. He is noble and kind and brilliant, like some kind of character left out of a Narnia book.

Nate is completing an album with a new band, including a couple of songs which have even morphed from The Halo Album That Wasn't. I'm listening to rough mixes now. I feel jealous and sad that I won't be a part of this release, almost as if I didn't see something through that I should have. At the same time I'm smiling, thinking of Nate playing me the demos in his car while trying to park his Arizona car on New York City's streets, his fender banging into the vehicle in front of us and his cigarette ashing on my arm.

The truth is that I never expected to meet these guys, these mismatched brothers. The kid with the beard and the boy with elfin hair. I don't think that they've even fully processed how much they've done together, how much they've accomplished and against what odds. It's too soon for that sort of tallying up.

I think tonight I will let the band go and allow myself to dream about the boy, about the things that he might have seen and done. And about how empty my arms felt as I pulled his waterlogged body from the pool. It might be a good moment to grieve for something more important than the songs that spilled out of the heads of two kids from Phoenix, no matter how important they have been to us all.

What a difference a year makes.

as filthy as a gay man on a saturday night

John is sitting across from me, sobbing. Broken. He has had his wallet and money stolen. For the past three hours he has been sleeping on the street, only to be woken when someone stole the last possession in his pocket, a pack of Marlboro Lights. This all is my fault because last night I took him to Amerika, a place where you can have the best night of your life. Or the worst.

Amerika is an astonishing club in Buenos Aires. It is full of sweat and sin. Over two thousand people pack into the space on weekend nights, taking full advantage of an open bar that comes included in the ticket price. Bartenders drip with perspiration as they dump 40-ouncers of Budweiser into crunchable plastic cups, pop countless bottles of champagne and pour shots directly into the mouths of alcohol-happy Porteños. The perimeter of the dance floor is surrounded by a drainage duct, in which busboys dump half-empty drinks and hose vomit. All the while a crowd loses its collective mind.

The idea was simple. My new friend and I would have a crazy night out. I had met John ("Can" is his real name, but it translates from Turkish as "John") in Spanish class. He was twenty six and came to Argentina from Istanbul, having just split up with his long-time girlfriend and recently telling his family that he was gay. "My mother cried. She said that I am just depressed and I could not possibly like dick."

He explained that rump-roasting is not taboo in Turkey. It is not uncommon for straight men to have sex with transvestites or gay men – the definitive rule being that if you're on top, you're straight, no matter what you're dipping into. In a culture where straight men are banging gay men for pleasure, I can see why it would be confusing to figure out just where your preferences lay.

We took a taxi to Palermo, and then waited in line with a straight couple who had gotten a babysitter and taken the night off from the misery of a screaming baby. I asked them if they knew that the bar was mostly gay. "Yes but it's okay. We like it because we can forget that we are parents and sometimes we forget to be dirty and sexy. So we come here. Nobody is more, how you say, *filthy* than the gays."

Fifty pesos later, John and I entered the main hall. A man dressed like Charlie Chaplin was swinging overhead on a trapeze, as a remixed classic Madonna track blared from the perfect sound system. Thousands of bodies grinded and cheered as the beat took a less pop direction, moving into a chicka-chicka beat and away from The 80's. It wasn't dull house music but it was no longer a familiar hit – the DJ knew what was designed to propagate lust and chaos, as if all the previous music had just been a warm up. Amerika went off.

A drag queen who could have been mistaken for Iggy Pop howled and swung his hair wildly. Arms reached over shoulders for drinks at the bar. Girls with lit cigarettes flailed their arms, like Medusas with a nicotine habit. People were dancing anywhere that there was room – on top of podiums, on the stage and on couches. We played our part, consuming dangerous house vodka and gossiping about the people in the crowd. Iggy Pop came over and danced for us, his cheap red heels accentuated by varicose veins and emaciated legs. "Whooooooooooooooooo," he would say after every tenth beat of the music. "Whoooooooooooooooooooooooo."

The smoky dance floor eventually pushed us upstairs, to an area called the Love Tunnel. In most circles it's simply referred to as a Dark Room, an area of a club where people congregate to slam bodies. I squeezed into a curtained-off area about the size of a basketball court, the air still thick with thumping beats. It was 4:30am, which seemed to be the peak time for getting some action.

A sea of people were mounted against walls, down on their knees or riding their partner on one of the many couches. Every combination of body parts was in play; dick on dick, dick on vagina, dick in mouth of person with dick in vagina. The sound of condoms ripping was audible. There was one woman who obviously thrived in this environment, hanging herself face-first over the balcony while men lined up to take their turn with her. Guys would text their friends, letting others know that there was an easy lay on the balcony. Tourists downstairs were pointing camera phones at the spectacle from below, surely collecting imagery that even the filthiest porn sites had not yet imagined.

John and I split up to check out the action. I became aware that a Porteño was cruising me hard, eventually sliding up beside me and putting my hand on his crotch, which contained a piece so large that it should not have been inserted in anything smaller than the eye of a hurricane. I took a pass. Minutes later I saw the same cruiser in a corner with an eager taker. I was unable to stop watching as something the size of a policeman's bayonet went in and out of his partner's mouth. He looked at me and smiled, as if saying, "this could have been you."

I continued to wander the dimly lit room and took it all in. Like the man servicing a crowd of five other guys. I strolled by one couch where a straight couple was quietly doing The Nasty. I was surprised when the man waved at me, then put his hand on the woman's waist as he regained his stride. It was the couple from line.

Eventually I found John and told him that I was probably going to leave. "I will stay and take a taxi home myself." His shirt was ripped open, his hair was sweaty and he had the crazy look of a cat in front of a bowl of guppies. I told him to be careful and text me when he got home.

No text arrived and I assumed that he had pulled. By noon I became worried and called his phone, which was shut off. I signed onto Facebook and saw that his profile had been dormant for 18 hours. Suddenly, an instant message popped up from John. "I am so fucked." He recounted his evening.

He had been fleeced of his wallet and cell phone while making out with a guy in the Love Tunnel, not realizing it before it was too late. He asked the club to call the police and they simply kicked him out. He slept on the street next to the club where, at 8 a.m., a bouncer tossed his empty wallet into his lap. An employee then took pity on him and gave him 20 pesos to get home, at which point John realized that his keys had also been stolen. A locksmith was called and two hours later, he was broke. I bought him dinner that night and he looked like a man who had run two marathons.

He told me the story over and over, a man in shock. He eventually worked through the other side of the trauma, emerging a deranged champ. "Can we go back next weekend?"

obama day

The Expatriates of Buenos Aires all came together at a club called Sugar for the purpose of seeing Barack Obama sworn in as the 42nd president. The divey club in Palermo was having a Moment, having marketed their venue as the only place to see the event live, with superior sound and on a big screen. As it turned out, the operation was really a jerry-rigged computer projector, with a herky-jerky picture and intermittent sound. Anderson Cooper's normally-competent voice came through at intervals. "Arriving in the. And here you can see. For which we have all been waiting."

Nobody seemed to care that they were watching the event on a setup that rivaled those found in most adult movie emporiums. The room was crammed with people who all had one thing in common; they'd fled America, short term or long term. A majority of the permanent residents seemed to have left post-Clinton, none of them imagining then that they would eventually bump into a president who promised to unite the country, if not the world. They were Bush-haters, thrilled to have a big 'ol target on which to blame their problems.

"America had gone the way of chain restaurants. It was McAmerica", explained Bill, a former engineer from Georgia, who was slurping down a Budweiser and munching on chicken wings. He then broke into a diatribe I have heard many times. It involved him recalling things that he remembered before The United States had gone tits-up, things that were almost placed memories, romantic visions that existed for the purpose of justifying his geographic displacement.

Imagine, for a minute, an antique Coca-Cola vending machine. The old-fashioned kind that dispensed small, adorable bottles for a nickel. We've had this image placed into our brains mostly through advertising, or at least from a film studio's clever prop department. It is an image that feels incredibly American - an image that reeks of small town comfort. The truth is that you may have probably only run into a handful of these in your life, most likely in a setting where they are intended to be flashback-y and kitsch. You're not foolish enough to believe the world would be transformed if we could still plop down a nickel for a miniature soda. But I really think this is the deluded, romantic vision that guys like Bill are holding onto. He had left America in search of things that never really existed in his own life, things that he was convinced would make himself happy.

I recently had dinner with a former New Yorker, who was now living in Buenos Aires. He rolled his eyes as he explained that many Expats were thinking of returning to the USA now that Bush was leaving office. He said, "They are the same despicable poseurs who will threaten to leave when anything rocky happens here." As I began talking to more folks at Sugar, it indeed seemed this way.

Barbara left America after her husband cheated on her, leaving her a stockpile of cash awarded by an "asskicking judge." In Argentina she found that her money went further, healthcare was usually free and she could make dough by fact checking for a United States based company. Now, she said, things were changing. Inflation was approaching 35 percent a year and little things were starting to nag at her. "I miss salad dressing. I know that sounds stupid. But they don't make it here – you cannot find a bottle in the grocery to save your life." Barack Obama and Thousand Island were promise enough for her to consider a move back to Kentucky.

Every inch of free space at Sugar was jammed with news cameras, looking for easy pickup shots that they would use to cut into the nightly news. Several seats were reserved for journalists, men in sandals and jeans who ate nachos with such ferocity that I could only imagine their first below-the-belt encounter with a female. Behind me sat the two girls that I've been trying to avoid for all of my traveling life;

sorority sisters from Tennessee. "This is like, so monumental. All of my African American friends are like, so proud."

The telecast proceeded as I had anticipated it would. There was hissing when W was announced for his last puzzled-looking image as a president. The crowd's fury turned to pandemonium as Obama made his way to the screen. It felt more like watching Hulk Hogan enter a wrestling ring than it did a president approaching a podium. Then, thankfully, there was silence as he was sworn into office.

The moment did not provide the chills that I'd wanted it to and I wondered if this was because I was not in America, surrounded by people who had no choice but to slug through the next four years of turmoil. I was instead surrounded by people who had made a life outside of The United States and held some kind of secret remorse with this decision. Their quality of life had improved but they had traded their American soul in return. These were people who were constantly looking to justify their decision and maybe, just maybe, the man on the screen in front of them was going to make America a better place than where they currently sat. Which would make them very wrong about many things. It felt like they wished it hadn't happened.

yaqueta island, fiji

The transfer boat is tiny, leaks, is manned by a man with 32 consonants in his name and has no life preservers. It is a death ship. It pulls off land and for the next thirty minutes we alternate between horizontal and vertical, depending on which wave is most determined to flip us. Everyone turns green. Then, like magic, I am on Yaqueta Island.

I picked this island because it was off the books. Upon arrival a quick glance proved that the tip I'd been given was right; this is more of an outpost than anything else. I didn't expect anyone else to be here, but am greeted by one other tourist who was happy to see new company.

John is 22 year old Asian American from Connecticut. He has zero percent body fat and a six pack, presumably from training for every Olympic sport simultaneously.

Let me explain the 'resort.' There are seven leaky shacks on a beach, none with electricity and all with spiders the size of Pam Anderson's left tit. We live in shack number two which has ten bunk beds. My bed is seven millimeters from John's and I worry that my body fat will encroach onto his perfectly sculpted frame. He is Men's Health and Fitness, and I am the TGI Friday's Menu.

There is a pillow on my bed made of cast iron and a sheet that was woven by people without fingers. There is nothing comfortable about Yaqeta. Yet ten minutes later I am snorkeling and seeing the same fish that I only usually witness in my stoner friends' aquariums.

John and I eat some potato-ramen combo and drink bottled water that has been refilled and sold as if it is new. The generator runs out around nine. I take an Ambien to block out the mosquitoes buzzing around my bed's shoddy net and sleep blissfully until the End Of The World rain starts pummeling our hut at 6 a.m., just an hour before the breakfast conch has been blown with great inexperience. After seven trumpeted notes of what sounds like a dying ferret, John echoes my thoughts. "We get the point."

John has been alone on the island for two days and follows me around like a retriever. He is in the Navy ROTC, speaks military talk ("copy that") and I make a mental note to get him drunk and ask what really happens when sailors are at sea for months. I have seen porn with this theme and hope it is just as good.

We go to the village with Michael, who takes care of our resort. There are huts and roosters and dogs and kids running around and nobody is speaking anything other than Fijian. I only understand "bula," which means hello.

We visit a school and see knives stuck in coconuts, sleeping adults lying face first on the floor and a large color picture of Cher. There appear to be lessons about Japan on a chalkboard. The board reads, "The Japanese are rich. They live in big houses."

We leave the school and I nearly run into a cow that looks like Al Gore. Our eyes lock and the beast knows. "Oh Christ, not the Al Gore thing again."

On the way back we stop at the funeral of a woman who was 92. She is being buried in the sand and all of the kids are tossing dirt on her. I am asked to toss dirt on her. Then I am asked to help shovel dirt on her. I am burying a 92 year old Fijian woman.

I walk back to the resort with an older man who tells me that he has a mole. I tell him that's nice. He turns to show me something resembling a puss-filled red golf ball on his chest. I hold back the vomit and expect him to be dead in hours. He just shrugs and keeps walking. If I had a mole like that I would have 50 people praying for me in the ICU at St

Vincent's. This dude, he's gotta go take care of the goats now.

Everything gets surreal after this. The rain doesn't stop. Michael wants us to go to the village for lunch. We agree. When we arrive the village is in full funeral party mode. I say hi to Al Gore on the way in and he gives me a nasty look.

We watch men pound cava root (boring). We watch men drink cava root (boring). We sit on fly-covered blue tarps while the men talk about the dead lady in Fijian for an hour (sorry lady but booooooooooooooring). Then we sit in a man's fly-filled hut while he tries to push pork on me, which is only made worse by the fact that the pig's head is staring at me from outside the hut all cut off the body and dead-like and stuff.

John and I beg to be let out of this Fijian hell and start toward the beach, imagining how much fly poo each of us has had deposited on our skin. Then I see it. It was not something I was ready for.

They are slaughtering Al Gore.

He's moping around slowly as his belly is falling out. The crowd around him seems glad that he is dying. He falls. And then Al Gore is dead, tied to a stake by his feet and carried off. I skip the festival of death and return to the huts.

John and I play cards with the newly arrived Brits, who greatly resemble The Ropers. Joe, the husband, has been sick. That kind of sick. This will be Joe's last trip around the world. His wife is incredibly fun and upbeat and wears a tie-die sarong and tells me about seeing Pink Floyd at the first Glastonbury Festival. I'm hoping she will adopt me. I want to live with her in Bath and go down to the pub with her every day and have a discreet relationship with a man named Philip who will either work at the steel mill or the local arts and crafts store. Several whiskies later the generator runs out. John and I stumble to our bunkroom.

But here's the thing.

I have to jack off. I mean really, I have not gone this long since I was 15 years old. John is asleep or maybe listening to headphones. I am buzzed on the Jack Daniels we've been drinking and I just don't care any more. I consider a trip to the bathroom to take care of it but can't shake the image of a snake coiling around my dick in the dark like a venomous cock ring. Also it is dark in the room and I have the mosquito net around me and it operates as a wall. This is how I rationalize things when I have this much semen inside of me.

I do this wristy thing because I can't rapid-move with John so close. It's more of a slow movement, with subtle flare and major style points at pivotal moments. I make fast work of it. Four things happen quite quickly. 1) I blast buckets and buckets. 2) I suppress the biggest moan of my life so far on this planet. 3) I look around overwhelmed with the amount of fluid, unsure of what protocol is. 4) I fall asleep.

I wake up at dawn, looking at two semen drips hanging from the mosquito net, sort of semi-crystalized from the hours that have passed. The morning sunrise is hitting them at an angle that can only be described as beautiful. An orgasm stalactite.

I wake to my last day on Yaqueta. We have seven hours to kill between breakfast and the boat transfer. There is nothing to do. I pace the beach and Energy Boy climbs a rock, building further muscle mass. We eat and then climb into the boat. John is going back to Connecticut and I am on to a new island. We are both very excited to leave Yaqueta behind us. Also we've been talking about pizza and John has that near-narcotic extra-cheese look in his eye. Then it all goes wrong.

The sound of a boat engine dying is not very dramatic. A couple of pings, a sputter. We drift. We use a pole to get back to the beach. We nearly cry. We will miss the Big Boat.

We are angry. We stew. We do not say thank you when they upgrade us to a hut with its own bathroom and wasps that co exist in the ceiling with mice. This will be a miserable night.

John takes what he calls an "angry swim" and I hike an hour to the top of the mountain, because I heard if you do two back-flips while praying you can get cell service. No luck. Just goats who run away so fast they fall down, probably because you are throwing rocks to get them off the path. I contemplate putting my Blackberry into an apple juice bottle and setting it out to sea, my last plea for help as the island sucks my soul into its sand. I've gone to a Morrissey level of melodrama.

John and I collect loads of wood. Our concept is that the only thing that will make us happy now is a fire that "you can see from Mars." The locals look at us like we are nutso, as we discuss how we don't know if bamboo will burn but gee doesn't it look just like the sake containers at Nobu. Everything we pile onto the fire burns big and bright.

Our transfer boat works the next day and we make the Big Boat on time. We laugh, relieved.

I say goodbye to John. I know how this goes. We exchange email addresses and make claims to keep in touch, but won't. For three days and four luxurious nights we were best friends. We would never have even talked to each other if we met in the airport. Because of circumstance we had some moments in the past few days that will probably age as well as those with my best friends. It's not every week you get stranded on an island, watch a presidential nominee get slaughtered and light a fire that you can see from Mars.

coming up in ubud and down in kuta

Anyone who has ever taken ecstasy will tell you that it is impossible to plan for when it will hit. It's up to the purity of the drug, the environment and your general mental state.

I'd been waiting for this trip to hit me. To "come up." I thought for sure it would be scuba diving The Reef, skydiving in Sydney or chilling on the beach in Seminyak. But it never hit until tonight, in Ubud. Bammmmmmmmm, just like when E hits. A force that knocks your knees out from under you and leaves you hanging there, floating above where your toes just were.

Here is what I now understand about this trip.

The unplanned stops are going to be better than the planned ones. The low points are going to be lonely. I have figured out that I need to stop steering my course so accurately and pick left when it feels better than right, even if right has air conditioning and blowjobs. I need to take chances that I would never conceive at home. I need to miss New York in a devastating way before I can go back.

I can't put my finger on why *this* is the place, but if you're a traveler then you will understand. Sometimes you unexpectedly pause in a spot that feels right. At that point, either everything goes absolutely right or terribly wrong. Even when it goes wrong, you have a great story.

Inevitably, I guess, my comedown was horrible.

My last day here was ruined when a boy drowned in the hotel pool. There is no Meredith Grey here. I watched the staff pull his lifeless, face-down body from the water after other sunbathers started pointing at him. The unsuccessful CPR was not followed by emergency helicopters or vacationing doctors with miracles. Just death. A little boy, dead. I am still trying to shake the screams and cries of the parents, which drove me to my room. Their life is clearly over. I am sure that I should be writing more about this but I just can't. It was a horrible thing to have seen. And now, five hours later, there are 50 people laughing and swimming in the pool.

singapore and the gum thing

Anyone who knows me will tell you one thing about me: I hate when people chew gum. Specifically, I despise when mouths chaw, gnarl and mangle objects. A combination of this with bubble snapping is enough to push me to the boundaries of sanity. It's a problem.

I decided to make a pit stop in Singapore because it is still the only place that gum is unlawful. This was my Holy Land. This was my Jesus Christ.

Gum 101: The horrors of gum chewing began with the Greeks and Aztecs, who chewed on tree resin as a form of oral pleasure. An official formula was patented in 1869, finding its way into the first gumball machines two years later. William Wrigley souped up the recipe with mint extracts in 1914. Frank Fleer was the real gum guru, creating Blibber-Blabber in 1906 (the first bubble gum).

Fortunately for me, there is Singapore. Gum was banned in 1992, after vandals began sticking it on the sensors of the prized Mass Rapid Transit. Here's the best part: Nobody missed it. No black market ever developed, even though offenders were only "named and shamed" if caught – which is not even a slap on the wrist by Singapore standards. Prime Minister Lee Kuan Yen commented at the time, "If you can't think because you can't chew, try a banana."

The resurfacing of legal gum in Singapore is an excellent example of just how bizarre and corrupt America can be. In 1999, desperate to open bilateral trade with Bush's USA, the government agreed to two things. The first was public support for the war in Iraq. The second was repealing the gum ban. That's quite a dick sucking, in terms of trade negotiation.

There was, of course, a back-story. The year before, Wrigley's had hired a lobbyist who then leaned on an Illinois congressman to put gum on the Bush Agenda. Only the devil knows what was traded in making this a sticky issue for Singapore, who picked up a 150 million dollar tax break per year on their end of the deal.

However, the government in Singapore found a crafty way to save face. Some gum has medicinal purpose, even if is to help build enamel or fight cavities. Therefore, they made gum an item that must be handed out by pharmacists, only after taking down the names of customers for a national record. Any importing of gum is still illegal. There is something perversely exciting to me about this. I could buy a parrot at 4:30 a.m. in Manhattan but a person in Singapore must ask a pharmacist for a stick of Hubba Bubba.

For the past five days I have not seen a single person chew gum. No whorish women snapping their cud. No athletes mouthing the sticky substance like it was their junior prom date. I have had beautiful, thoughtful moments without the presence of my nemesis. And nobody – not even the spoiled tourists – seems to miss it.

I propose a gum free world. If I had a billion dollars I would buy lobbyists and make it a priority. Until then, I will have Singapore.

cameron highlands, malaysia

Tanah Ratah is a particularly ugly town in an extraordinarily beautiful setting. It sits smack-dab in the middle of the Cameron Highlands, a crisp and cool area of Malaysia that supplies enough tea for the whole country. The tea plantations are mostly owned by a Scottish family, who has made a killing by hiring locals at .20r per kilo of tea picked. Sweat shops in fields.

The place has a laid back feel, but not in a hippy-mystical sort of way. Eyesores like the abandoned development in the center of town are forgotten when you look at the hills, while sipping a cup of tea or eating a local strawberry.

My first accommodation choices were booked and I randomly stumbled upon Papillion, a small guesthouse set back a superhero's stone throw from town. The owners are about the nicest people you will ever meet and my room was perfect, with the added indulgence of a hot shower.

It was in Tenah Ratah that I realized how vitally different the races inhabiting this country are. The predominant split is between the Chinese and Islamic factions, who seem to talk about each other behind closed doors, yet are all smiles in public. I rode by an apartment for let with which specified "for Chinese only" at the bottom of the sign. Food stalls next to each other waft a conflicting mix of curry and stir-fry.

There is the attempt to present this culture as "Malaysian" but it has been obvious through my travels that there is no such thing, only symbiotic factions who live in the same place. Yet there is no hint of upheaval or conflict, as with many countries in the same situation.

Truth be told, sightseeing here is littered with tourist traps, all trying to sell you what is displayed on the tour. There are berries at farms, tea at plantations and honey from hives. I spent one day touring them all and that was plenty. The real treasure here lays in the nooks and crannies.

The shining example of the vibe here is T Cafe, where I ate every day. The owner's six year old served as hostess during the afternoon, ushering me to a seat in a way that almost made me interested in having kids. "You sit, you eat, you love!" Postcards from people who remembered it fondly lined the room. I've never had service that felt as genuine before and the owner is greatly flattered when you return for the third time, almost to the point of being embarrassed. Her look says "but we really don't do anything THAT special here." They do.

I spent my mornings playing with Max The Puppy and my nights tossing wood on the bonfire at Daniel's Guesthouse, where a dozen backpackers gathered each night to swap stories. The nights were chilly and I stayed close to the fire, even when the wind changed direction and blew smoke in my face. Each morning I woke up smelling a bit like a fireplace.

I had one notable encounter while in town, writing at a corner bar. A 20-something guy ripped me out of my writing trance, asking me if he could sit down and have a beer. I had the sense that I was being hit on and I was right. His name was Ryan, a Filipino living here for two years, studying hotel management. He pointedly asked me if I liked boys or girls and I coughed up the boy answer, outing myself to the only gay for miles. He said he had been watching me for two days and I heard a tone in his voice that concerned me - absolute loneliness.

It had been two years since he had sex in this largely Islamic town and several since he'd had a magical kiss. I began to catch a tone that unsettled me, the "take me away from here" thing that I have encountered before in other small towns. Ryan had been daydreaming about me and I think he had swept himself up into a fantasy that I was The One, or at least A One. I created a story about a boyfriend back home in order to sidestep a dream-crushing. His face fell but he continued to work me over, offering that he found white guys "delicious." I couldn't break it to him that I found white guys delicious too and had no urgings for men of the Flip variety. Better to let him think that Mike The Banker was the reason for my below-the-belt indifference.

We had a couple of beers and I left before his small town sadness could seep into the pleasant buzz that this town was giving me. Anyone looking for a nice Flip guy, just park yourself at the corner bar here and make yourself known. Also, they are probably lying about there being no tap beer, so they can nab an extra two Ringit for a bottle. Raise an eyebrow and you'll get your pint.

I am sitting in the yard, writing this with *In Rainbows* on my headphones and Max chewing on the lace of my shoe. Three nights in Tanah Ratah has been just right. Tomorrow I head back to Kuala Lumpur, where I have splurged on a luxury hotel room. It may be another solo Valentine's Day but at least I will be dreaming in sheets with a thread count higher than my IQ.

notes from vietnam

There is this squatting thing that people do in this part of the world. Usually the person is steeped on a curb, feet on the edge, chilling the hell out. There is no muscle quiver, spasm or give. They can squat like this for hours. I see hundreds of people a day like this. Not impressed? Go ahead - try it. Stand in the middle of your room and squat, keeping your ass about one inch from the ground. Try it for ten minutes. Imagine staying like this for an hour. Then call Jenny Craig.

This is just one of a thousand differences I have found between Vietnam and America. There are no spinning classes or McDonalds or air conditioner repair shops. There are no public libraries or subways or Doppler weather forecasts. No gutters, baristas or professional clowns. Jobs that Westerners have created still serve no function here. I spent the better part of fifteen minutes trying to explain what a Dog Catcher was to a semi-English-speaking waitress who was fascinated with The American Way. "But why you want catch dog? Dog go when he ready."

In fact, the only universal thread I can seem to find is video games. Internet stores are jammed from 4-6 p.m. with kids desperate for an hour of dance simulation or first person murder. Video games. It seems that the only way to world communication maybe be between an online bullet battle between Nguyen in Sapa and Michael in Fort Wayne.

The most important job in Vietnam is not President or Oil Tycoon. It is Cook or Motorbike Repair Man. The jobs that are given value are the ones that actually keep society functioning. Bus Driver is high on the pyramid. Not only is this the main form of long-haul transport but it is also an incredible challenge, given that the highways here are really just byways. You can count the number of daily domestic flights on two people's hands. You couldn't count the number of buses. Period.

Here are some things I have seen on my bus ride today: A family of four on one motorbike with a tarp over their heads (rain shower). Cows in the front yard of a one bedroom house. An overturned motorbike with a crowd and a body on the ground. A fifty year old crane pulling a piece of bridge into the air with what looked like silly string. A monkey in a cage. A wedding in a field. Foggy roads that go into the sky and come out the other side of heaven.

Vietnam gets a bad rap on the Southeast Asia travel circuit and it probably deserves it. There seems to be quite a bit of crime committed against tourists here - crime that the people would not commit on their fellow countrymen, mostly because it's not as lucrative. Drive-by pickpocketing is prevalent in Nha Trang, especially at night when the bars let out. Hanoi is Scam City, with taxi drivers pulling shit that I have never even heard of before (and I once had a NYC cab driver masturbate while looking at me in the rear view mirror). The constant deluge of potential grubbing can get you down some days, especially if other travelers' stories begin to stack up.

The thing is, you just can't feel the hand of government here. There is not enough paper to push. Perhaps this is why the country lags between so many social structures. Ho Chi Minh is revered everywhere as a communist who united the people against the French and Japanese. Yet capitalism is everywhere - it is just a matter of time before the Starbucks and Gaps come to town. It's this confusion that makes the government seem invisible. With no desperate need to show The Vietnamese Way as The Right Way, it is left to quietly do the basics of what government needs to do. Like build bridges, build schools and get the people through to next year.

Overall, enough is more. Chess on the ground suits most people in the evening. There is no dying wish for a trip to The Mall or a $200 bar bill at a fancy hotel, and it would not even occur to anyone here as an option. The American Dream has become getting fired and paid out, in order to start a new life (where eventually we will long to be fired again). The Vietnamese Dream, at least for now, continues to be just getting through one life, not three.

Some days I look around and try to comprehend that I am here. Right now I am only 50km from jungle that is laced with undetonated mines and fields that have still not recovered from napalm. I wonder how unearthly a place this was to fight a war and then wonder again if a desert is much better. I see orphaned kids with deformities and healthy kids with school uniforms and backpacks. The West is creeping into this country but from where I stand it still feels foreign and remote.

This country isn't simply sewn up. Vietnam is teetering on the edge of two millenniums and I am lucky enough to be right here during this middle moment, at a cafe in Dalat, drinking cherry tea.

the underdog

I wasn't even thinking of eating dog until I met Alec. He had a way of smiling and raising his eyebrows that suggested trouble, the kind of trouble that I just had to get into.

Alec was German. He could have been my boyfriend if he didn't have a girlfriend. He giggled at my unspoken jokes (a nod at a kid picking his nose) and spoke excellent English. Alec was also insanely hot, a triathlete who still drank enough beer to not be featherweight but carried enough muscle to have a tight, convex chest.

During our first drink, he told me about the time when he cheated on his girlfriend back home. It had been after a long bus ride through Laos, during which a beautiful girl had suggested they seek accommodations together. After dinner and drinks they headed to her room. Just before they started making out he felt a bit sick but his hormones got the best of him and he forged ahead. Halfway through the act, with her on top, he began having severe gastric pains. She thought he was getting more turned on and thrashed harder and faster, which made him offer a clenched whimper. At that point, Alec confessed, "I shit on bed." This made him my best friend for life.

"You know. We should go for dog."

We were out at a balcony bar drinking whiskey at four in the afternoon when he offered it up, straight from the ol' Lonely Planet. I could only hear Anthony Bourdain whispering in my ear not to be a wimp, not to be the safe American consumer. I agreed to eat man's best friend. Alec was thrilled. I was thrilled to thrill him.

Our drinking continued into the evening with free beer on the roof of our hostel, the well-run, Australian-owned Hanoi Backpackers. Alec looked at me and tried to speak code as we batted off two frumpy Polish girls who would not stop hitting on us.

Alec. Giving me the accent. "Time for D-O-G now?" Certainly.

We hailed a taxi and headed to a decidedly sketchy neighborhood near the airport. It's a universal rule that no good comes of establishments near an airport. There were no people, no cabs, no stores and no cyclos, only a semi-fancy shack. "Dog!", said our driver pointing to the entrance. "Woof Woof."

The anxiety of eating Lassie was quadrupled by the shocking neighborhood and certainty that we would never get home. That feeling worsened when we realized that there were about ten canines wandering below the eatery's ten empty tables. The reality that dog came from DOG was almost too much. Bourdain kept whispering in my ear, cooing me closer to the tables. Before I knew it, my shoes were off and I was sitting at a Japanese style table on the floor. It bears repeating that Alec and I were the only customers.

Two men served as our cook and waiter. They looked more like mechanics more than restaurateurs. Between the two of them, they knew three words and gracefully laid out the dining options. "Boy Dog? Girl Dog?" We shrugged our shoulders and told them to pick what they wanted. Not understanding a word of what we said, they moved quickly towards the back. Chef's Special it was.

I worked in a rib joint once and it is best that the customer never knows what really happens behind the door that swings both ways.

Dinner arrived before we could even think about bailing out. Two small plates of grilled dog were placed in front of us, with three equally mysterious dipping sauces. The meat was brown and rump-like, chunked and sliced. The smell coming off of it made me momentarily gag. The dogs continued to whimper beneath the floorboards.

Our two hosts were now watching to make sure we partook. I grabbed my chopsticks and shoved a piece in my mouth before I really had time to process what I had in front of me.

Dog was a completely new and distinct taste to me. It had never struck me that at my age I might discover a new taste. It was like the first time I tasted licorice or lemongrass or coriander. Except more horrible than anything I had ever eaten in my life. Years of Liver Night as a kid had taught me how to convincingly fake-eat with a quick napkin spit, which is exactly what I did. Unlike in my childhood, the dogs under this floor would probably not appreciate my palmed scraps.

"Boy dog," said our waiter as Alec took a bite from the same stinking pile. Some people turn green - he turned neon green. Our waiter departed and he hacked out his bite into a napkin.

We should have stopped right there but we didn't. Neither one of us was leaving until we successfully downed one piece. We both went for the other sliced pile and I guess that I can compare the taste of female dog as something pork-like. It was only half as bad as the first pile, which was ten times worse than anything I have ever had. We swallowed. Dog had been ingested. We pounded our orange sodas and looked at each other with grim faces.

There was no pride in the achievement. We were just two dumb guys doing something for the sake of saying that we did it. Neither one of us enjoyed a single second of the experience and neither one of us felt good about what we had done. We had psyched ourselves into doing something because it felt adventurous and non-touristy. It was a horrible mistake and a nasty decision.

We paid quickly and left as if it was a brothel, wandering for an hour before finding a cab back to the city. It charged us three times the going rate and neither one of us cared. We just wanted the night behind us. We deserved to be ripped off.

homestayin'

I arranged a homestay through the travel agent in Chau Doc, Vietnam. Uncertain of what I had just negotiated and booked, I boarded a bus for My Tho. Three hours and one Crocodile Farm visit later I had arrived in town.

I was met by a beautiful young woman wearing a pink and black sweater and white furry gloves. It was eighty degrees but I knew that this is how people dress for long motorbike rides - you never know when the weather or your vehicle will break down. She introduced herself in Vietnamese as Hanh and then spoke seven sentences that I did not understand in the slightest. Smiling and nodding, she grabbed my pack and put it on the bike between her knees. I strapped my daypack over my shoulder, put on a helmet and jumped on the seat behind her. We flew out of the dirt lot at light speed.

Wide bridges and wide roads became narrow bridges and narrow roads. There was no communication between us, other than nervous laughs as we went over bumps or nearly died crashing into oncoming vehicles. Somewhere in those seven sentences she probably told me that the trip would be forty minutes long but I was fucked if I knew how long it would be. I had a horrible itch on my nose but dared not take my hands off of Hanh's shoulders, for fear of a bloody end.

Moving to dirt roads, we began to blow through villages as kids were being let out of school. They all pointed at us when we sped by. These people were used to seeing almost anything transported on motorbikes but we still turned heads – a tiny pink girl, a white man and one hefty backpack. This combination was about as improbable around here as seeing Scooby Doo nail Charlize Theron on a pool table.

We finally arrived at Hanh's house. My friend Glenn has a habit of calling accommodations "property" and I snorted at what his description would be. "It's, how shall I say, a rather modest property that has its own unique charm and atmosphere." It was a house on a river with a brick deck. It was exactly what I'd hoped to see.

Seven or eight people came to check out the arrival. Everyone talked about me while I was standing there, the syllables ricocheting through my head like buckshot.

I imagined what it would like to be airlifted into my own family and realized that it wouldn't be nerve racking, it would be downright frightening. My mother would be whizzing around with a 400 degree baking sheet of Fridays' Stuffed Mushrooms, my sister would be yelling at football players on the TV and other family members would be discussing how horrible the world was going to shit, I tell ya, you can't even go to Costco without running into goddamn Mexicans. This before Nana arrived with her nine plastic bags full of combs, Saltines, Sweet n' Low and yarn.

So this was a piece of cake.

I wrote for a while, in between playing with the puppy and eating a lunch of Elephant Ear Fish. Hanh took me up river for a boat trek and it felt like a reverse African Queen with her as Bogie and me as, well, The Queen.

A couple of the neighbor girls decided to show me off and take me up to the village. I eyeballed lots of the normal market goodies - squirming eels, flopping fish and dried squid. More Scooby Doo pointing from the locals. One boy said something unflattering about me as I walked by (I just knew it). I turned around and walked back toward him like only a New Yorker could, with severe attitude - he screamed and ran away. Little bitch.

The kids started taking baths at 6 p.m. This involved taking some shampoo to the river, stripping and jumping in. The grownups lifeguarded and the little ones wore life jackets, lest they drown or get eaten by crocodiles. Adults hit the river around seven. I even saw one guy hurl a bottle of shampoo across the entire river to his neighbor.

I spent the rest of the afternoon watching a man make a chair. This sounds mildly interesting until you really process that I mean *make a chair*. Home Depot had not contributed. He had found the appropriate pieces of bamboo and carved holes in them, carefully piecing together the interlocking parts. No bolts. No drills. No Ikea tools.

Night fell and I had a great dinner. Everyone sat on the deck and told stories but I only listened because they sounded like this:

"Neow tong mee kayartima chee chee yowl horra meeeeeee." Then laughter. I prayed that these were not tales of previous guests, all now kept chained in a pit.

Four French people showed up by boat around 10 p.m., looking for rooms. Their arrival ruined the whole balance that I had with the family. Worse still, they talked loudly and excessively. They spent a good deal of time ridiculing Vietnam.

My dreams were intense. I had popped my first pre-Laos anti-malaria pill and knew from a trip to Africa what would happen. I murdered the French people in my sleep.

I woke up at six and ate the same thing that has been served to me for the entire time I have been in this country - two eggs, a massive roll and the strongest cup of coffee you can imagine. The French were asleep and it was blissfully quiet on the river.

Hanh took me over the river and through the woods on her motorbike again. This time I recognized many of the kids from the previous day and they waved at me with a smile and familiarity.

"Hello Meester. Hello!"

from a flashpacker to a backpacker

The realization came at a guesthouse in remote Laos, the kind of place that miraculously hovers inches above the ground on concrete blocks. I was coming home from a night of desolation drinking. The generators had long since expired and I had only a flashlight to guide me.

A sleepless night on an inch thick mattress awaited me. The fan clanked with a unique beat, as if trying to keep up with some arcane drum 'n bass song that the big-pants people liked in the late 90's. I wasn't expecting to see the snake, curled up next to my bed.

"SNAKE! DO YOU SEE THIS? SNAKE! IS ANYBODY ELSE SEEING THIS?"

No one came running. No concierge, no guest-relations expert, no complimentary upgrade or oh-my-gosh-sir. I bravely threw *Three Cups Of Tea* at the reptile, pissing it off enough to do that thing where it revealed, yes, it could stand up too.

That night I slept in the unlocked room next door and decided, well, that's that. No more of this reptiles-under-the-bed nonsense. I would have to swallow my pride and become a Flashpacker.

And so it went for the rest of the year. I hunted online for mid-range deals, becoming an expert at finding better accommodations for 20 bucks more, happy to spend the extra dough in order to avoid the poop-smeared toilets at Hostel Incontinent-al. Hostels and teepees only became a viable option when everything else was sold out.

Then my day job went bye-bye, my 401k stopped growing and we all started loudly cursing airport taxes.

That extra twenty bucks a day had suddenly become more important to add to the survival kitty. Flashpacking went right out the window. I moved back to rooms with lime green paint jobs, roosters under the floorboards and showers with pervy peekholes.

I'm not alone. I've been away for three months and it's startling to see the adjustment that have taken place. Mid-level guesthouses, some only open a few months, look positively grim at night. There's no hiding the lack of occupants when only two rooms have lights on.

You'd think that this would encourage a shift in pricing but it's been my experience that they're holding onto that +$20 rate, playing a game that probably won't pan out in the long run.

On the other hand, cheapies are packed to the rafters and I've bumped into quite a few of my fellow former-midscalers along the way. We're all bargaining out here, happy to remind the owner that his "eco-tourist property" is really just a series of termite-ridden huts, and that his nightly solar-powered electricity will last only about as long as a good lay. We're politely elbowing for the room that faces the garden and violently face-masking for the bulkhead on flights.

I use hostel booking sites that don't require fees, rather than Expedia or Hotels.com. I find myself pillaging Kayak and Cheapflights for the best airfares, and then booking directly with the airlines so as to avoid their racking fees. I call airline reservation lines until I get the right agent, usually a wrinkled warhorse in Houston or Chicago. She will sometimes hit magical F keys and, after a pause that makes my heart pound, will come back with a "Well, would you look at that?"

These women (and lispy men named Charles) have been pulling backroom shenanigans for years and are often thrilled to speak with a system-scammer. We reminisce about the days of back-to-back Supersavers and how it used to be glamorous to work the counter at LAX.

I know which airline websites will charge me for baggage at the last click and which of their competitors won't. I've returned to train travel, knowing at least that I won't end up 30 miles from town and swallowing an unexpected twenty-dollar cab ride. I'm also reading all of the fine print, like when I discovered this week that my Eurail pass would snag me a £100 discount on the Eurostar.

This thriftiness has also made me savvy about things like travel insurance. I've spent hours comparing policies on insuremytrip.com and reading about other policies on message boards. I've pondered just how much each leg is worth, because every policy tends to pay out per limb lost.

You know what else? The cheapies are thrilled to see me again. They may not have painted the joint since Carter was president but they sure appreciate the business. Gone is the entitlement that follows a rave Lonely Planet review.

This isn't to say that high-end bargains aren't to be had. I recently caved and spent $100 for three nights in a Bangkok five-star. I locked myself in the room for days, thrilled to spend my CNN time with the nice kind of sheets. Checking into a guesthouse the night after, I felt ridiculous for having spent the money, but not for the time spent being seduced by Anderson Cooper's dreamy eyes.

Truth be told, I'm having a better time traveling now than I have in years. I'm writing this article from a 'splurge,' a riverside residence that sits just north of budget. A travel agent in Vientiane tried to sell me two nights here for $100, "breakfast included!" I pondered plunking down my Visa, and then walked outside to call the hotel directly. I got it for ten bucks.

it could have been a tuesday night in connecticut, except i was on a river in india

I went to Alleppey in order to scratch the itch of two childhood memories. Cruising the backwaters on a houseboat seemed like some kind of circle-of-life-y thing that I just needed to do.

The first memory was of riding The Jungle Cruise, an attraction that I begged to board during our annual family hell-cation to Disneyworld. My whining would begin in Hall of the Presidents and would not be snuffed until we'd rounded corner into Fantasyland. I was only happy when our very fake boat made its way down the even more fake chlorine river, passing the most fake animals.

My second memory is of watching *The African Queen*, a film that always seemed to be on our television. I never complained because it seemed to elevate my father's mood to the point where he might not snap. I saw this movie at least twenty times by the time I was ten, understanding even then that I was always going to be more of a Hepburn than a Bogie.

And so I went out in search of my own river adventure.

Booking a boat in Alleppey was a breeze. With over three hundred in circulation, I had my pick of the litter and decided on one that looked like a fancy bale of hay. It was an old-school model, propelled by a burly man holding a thirty-foot pole.

The newer ones looked a bit too South Beach in comparison, tricked out with motors, satellite dishes and flat screens. I figured that if you're going to float through canals on a piece of wicker, it might as well be on something authentic and flammable.

My hopes for a boozy staff were dashed when I met Captain Sensible, a stern man who obviously did not fancy nonsense. I managed to quickly get chummy with his partner Chef Bloodbath, who had just chopped a significant portion of his finger into my lunch.

The boat was surprisingly sturdy and was designed for the crew to hang out in the back (talking about the guests) and the passengers to hang out in the front (wondering what they're saying). I was the only guest.

My room contained a sun-faded picture of Jesus, the holes in his hands bleeding brown and his Russell Brand haircut turned some shade of dark blond. It made what was surely a bad day for him look even worse.

The twenty-hour trip did an excellent job of showing off the canals, some quite remote while others meandered through the backyards of local houses. During the first hour we passed concrete walls that were spray-painted with the communist sickle, a bird eating another bird, children screaming, women doing their washing and agitated roosters.

I grew antsy after a few hours, probably still expecting animatronic hippos to come popping out of the water. I came to realize that this is what they meant by "Slow Travel", a term surely invented by the kind of people who walk around with crocheted bags and nylon sandals.

Unable to naturally chill, I popped a Panadol and downshifted into the groove of the river, my ears doing that buzzy thing that happens when codeine hits the system. I began to have deep thoughts. Things like why ducks still swim, despite the fact that they can fly.

Captain Sensible parked the boat around six, at the end of what I guess was a aquatic cul-de-sac. A beautiful sunset transpired. Music began playing from something sounding like a bullhorn. Mosquitos undertook suicide missions. Parents sent their children out to purge their pre-bedtime energy. Men worked on their motors. Curious smells wafted from kitchens.

I spent the night eating a proudly prepared dinner, drinking Kingfisher and watching the lizard-things devour anything that approached the deck's lone light bulb. My newfound zen-ness relaxed even my thumbs, allowing me to defeat Bowser in a Nintendo DS battle that had been a long time coming.

I woke in the morning upon the advice of Bloodbath, who was at my door loud-whispering "Wake up." I rubbed my slept-in contact lenses deeper into my cornea and dragged myself towards coffee. The world had already woken up around me, everyone rushing to get to somewhere, either by boat or by path.

The journey ended rather abruptly. We poled our way back towards town, quickly reaching the departure dock. The crew jumped off the boat and scrambled toward the next guests, who were waiting to jump on. It was easy to see that the whole thing was going to be repeated with an endless loop of tourists, which is not so far from Disneyworld after all.

locked down at heathrow

dink: [di NG k] noun, slang. An irritating, contemptible individual.
Use: The customs officials that he encountered at Terminal Five were
a bunch of dinks.

"Don't worry. I'm not going to do anything crazy." His eyes told me that he was speaking the truth but it was the white rubber gloves that were scaring me. I've never seen a TV show where the guy in the white gloves just gives you a kiss on the cheek and a pat on the ass.

Plus, I'd just been fingerprinted and was standing outside of Heathrow's lockdown. I was much less concerned with where his fingers were headed and more worried about how I had ended up in the pokey.

I had come from Italy, where I'd taken a train all day, followed by a cheapo flight to the UK. About ten hours of travel. I had, as is geographically mandatory, walked 39 miles through Heathrow before arriving at the customs podium. I was exhausted, melancholy and quite ready to fall into the arms of my boyfriend, who was waiting for me in London.

"How long will you be here?" Oh, this crap. Couldn't they read the neatly printed "7 days" in the box of the same question? I noticed that his fingernails were manicured, which struck me as bit metro for such a tough guy gig. He thumbed through my passport, which was nearly full of stamps and visas.

"What are you doing here?" I'm a tourist. "What will you do when you're here?" I will go see Bruce Springsteen in Hyde Park, see a couple more concerts and visit with friends. "Who are your friends?"

I thought for a second about taking a philosophical approach and asking in return, "Yes, good point. Who *are* our friends?"

Instead I rattled off a few names, including Lewis'. I hoped that this gentleman wouldn't ask me about how I'd met Lewis, a story that involves caipirinhas and a make out session on a picnic table in Chile.

"I see here that you're a writer. What do you write?" I explained that I was a freelance travel writer. Officer Manicure asked if I did anything else, insinuating that this couldn't possibly be a real job. I explained that I didn't, and that I was making my way around the world for a year with this income.

He sucked air through his teeth and made his eyebrows go cross-eyed. "How much money do you have?" I told him about ten grand. That didn't seem like enough, based on his reaction. He abandoned his podium, directed me to heel and led me to collect my bags.

Along the way he told me there was probably no issue but the answers I'd given fit a profile similar to one of people who might disappear into the country. I explained that I was not fond enough of kebabs and greasy chips to stay in the UK. He laughed and assured me that we'd have this settled in no time. "I'm really jealous of what you're doing, this trip. I wish I could do it." He had the miserable look of somebody who took holidays on the English seaside.

My bags were searched, specifically for anything that would indicate I'd come to England forever. The good officer told me that often they find cards from going-away parties. He found my Western Europe Lonely Planet. "This is good. I'll be able to show them this and corroborate that you're on the trip you claim to be on." He confiscated all of my notebooks and my collection of receipts. "This is all good. It proves that you are who you say you are." It was a strange place to have an identity crisis.

I also produced my onward ticket, a flight to Spain. He did the air-sucking thing again and explained that thirty quid flights didn't stand as any kind of evidence for departure, because cheap flights could be abandoned. He lamented there might be some issue with my not having a return flight to America, even though I had a ticket out of the country.

I spent the better part of the next three hours in an intimidating questioning room. Everything in the 10×10 room was nailed to the floor, making me imagine just what maniac had started swinging chairs to initiate that protocol. I could see the other rooms through glass, both occupied with stressed-looking travelers being questioned for God Knows What. Manicure asked me about ten more questions, then asked if he could contact Lewis to corroborate my story. I agreed, hoping this would settle the entire thing.

My big problem came in the form of a change of the guard. I was assigned a new officer at 7 p.m. because mine was going home. A strange, shaky man, Officer Anxious regretted to tell me that he'd have to start at the beginning and ask me every question. Good cop, nervous cop. He took notes on cheap, ruled paper. His hyper eyes darted between the page and my face. Much less forthcoming than Manicure, he dropped me back in the main customs area and hustled off.

He returned with pursed lips. He regretted to inform me that I had been denied entry to the United Kingdom. He explained that they had spoken to Lewis and found a discrepancy between our stories. Lewis, not really knowing how to explain my history with a band we were gong to see, simply told them that I used to work with them as their manager, which was the truth. Anxious seized upon this and deduced that I was here to work with this band, to "market and promote."

I denied this over and over, yet I was branded a "doubtful entry" and a liar by the C.I.O (Chief Immigration Officer), which sealed my case. I was told that I should have immediately said I was in The UK to see a band that I formerly managed, even if it had nothing to do with my current job, and right when I walked into the customs area. Because I hadn't, I had lied. The logic sounded dicey to me too.

I've since recreated the behind-the-scenes events that took place, mostly from pieces of information the airport staff would later slip me in hushed voices. It should be said that this is purely conjecture. First, it seems that the C.I.O. went off duty with Manicure. The C.I.O. didn't feel like dealing with my issues and ordered me to be denied. When I complained to Nervous and asked to see a C.I.O., she was called at home because it was her case and then she really became pissed. "Not happy" is the British way of saying that.

I think, at this point, everyone was told to hang me up on absolutely anything they could. I've since learned that the folks at LHR can hang just about anyone up on something. There are just too many rules to pull from.

Eventually, I would hold paperwork that denied me entry because of my failure to indicate that I was working (completely untrue and never documented by anything I'd said), that my funds were insufficient (ten grand for one week) and that I didn't have a ticket back to America (although I had one for Spain).

Something happened to Nervous after he delivered the news. He began stuttering when speaking and I noticed his hands shaking. I remember thinking that somebody who has a good case wouldn't act like this.

It was here that I was searched and relieved of my possessions, including everything in my pockets except my phone. I was ushered into a room that contained 30 folding chairs, a TV and a ten foot stretch of bullet-proof glass, behind which I was observed by three officers packing heat. I was in jail.

I would flip between utter despair and total anger during the next eight overnight hours. One security guard, a surprisingly nice man in his mid-fifties who had "seen it all, mate" told me to accept my fate, that he'd only seen three people get themselves out of this situation and they all knew somebody in government. He'd heard about my case and shook his head. He would explain, after a few hours of conversation, about how the whole process worked, that I was probably marked an "easy pull." He wouldn't admit that there were quotas to meet but he did tell me that I looked like the kind of guy they "like" to refuse. In other words, I wasn't going to get physical or spit in anyone's face.

I phoned an immigration attorney who was absolutely shocked that this happened, and suggested that I petition to see a C.I.O. I did and was denied. They sent Officer Anxious instead, who met me with a determined look. He'd clearly been put in a terrible situation and tried to get stern with me, which just made him shake more. "Llllllllisten. Just accept it. You're gggggggggggoing home."

I wouldn't accept it and asked to see all of my paperwork. I asked them to strike several things that simply weren't true (they did) but was unable to have stricken that I was in the UK to work with this band. Their interpretation was the hook they'd hung me on and it wasn't going anywhere, no matter how untrue. Policy was in motion and they had the upper hand.

I was to fly at 8 a.m. and made one last appeal, this time with a morning shift officer who looked like Dusty Springfield. Officer Dusty came clean with one piece of new information. While speaking to Lewis, he'd also told him that we were going out. Although not something they were willing to put on my paperwork, it was something that they were holding against me.

Nobody had ever asked me about our relationship and it's never been my policy to offer that I'm gay to complete strangers; there are just too many closet homophobes in the world. Plus, in my post-Italy dazed state, it never even occurred to me that it would matter. I'd been through Heathrow at least 40 or 50 times before with not even a second glance.

Dusty claimed that I should have offered this news at the first podium when asked whom I was visiting. I said that I had, that I was seeing friends and listed Lewis' name. "But he's not just your 'friend.'" I got angry. "So let me get this straight. I was supposed to walk up to the podium and say that one of the reasons I'm here is to explore a relationship with another man? There are still quite a few homophobes left in the world." She didn't answer. There was a reason that this was left off the paperwork. She repeated the company line. "Just accept it."

At 8 a.m. I was 'whisked' through airport security by two guards. They had heard about my story, which was apparently making the rounds. One of the guards told me that my case wasn't uncommon and his partner coughed up a more surprising comment. "If I were you, I'd be kicking and screaming right now."

In perhaps the most embarrassing moment of my life, I was brought onto the plane in advance of all other passengers by security. My passport was handed to the head flight attendant, who was not allowed to give it to me until we landed. All of the other passengers pointed and whispered at me as they filed onto the plane, imagining what I'd done that could have landed me in this situation. Up until this point, I'd never so much as had a detention, let alone any kind of police escort.

I landed at JFK and sailed through customs. Two days later I'd booked a flight to Spain to rejoin my trip, at the cost of $1,400. I attempted to see somebody at the British Embassy in New York to discuss my case, only to be told the embassy does not see anyone about visa matters.

It was suggested that I get a lawyer who could figure out how to cut through the red tape of an appeal. I had a letter from the band's manager saying that I wasn't there to work and a lot of questions to ask someone but I couldn't afford to ask them – a lawyer was beyond my reach, especially after eating over a grand for new flights.

It turns out that I didn't need a lawyer. Two months later I went returned to the United Kingdom, this time through Edinburgh. I was prepared with every kind of evidence that I needed to prove that I was there to visit and attend the Fringe Festival and see Lewis, who I immediately offered was indeed my gay love interest, which made the older Customs Official blush terribly.

Although he did pull me out of line, he was polite, efficient and reasonable. I was a nervous wreck but he helped make me feel like a human again, just by his demeanor and the way he asked the questions. He asked to see my exit flight and bank statement, which contained less money than it had last time.

His eyebrows rose when he came upon my crossed out passport stamp from London. "Oh, Terminal Five." as if to say that it all made sense now. He then stamped my passport and welcomed me to the United Kingdom.

are you getting it? really getting it?

Traveling alone only begins to wear on me when The Thing happens. It is always brought on by not having spoken to people in days, often in areas where I just simply can't grasp the language (particularly countries where syllables like "yeoowowowowoweee" contribute greatly to an adverb). The Thing is simply this: One song gets in my head, loops and repeats for days.

You're probably imagining "Beautiful" by James Blunt invading your mind for a few hours while cleaning, or maybe whistling "Lady Marmalade" in the shower, eventually uttering "Geez, I wish *that* would stop." The frequency with which you replay this song is 1/100th of how often I will hear it and 1/1,000,000th of the duration it will stay stuck in the front of my mind.

Currently, The Thing is in high gear. The song in question is "Armageddon It," the fifth single from Def Leppard's multi platinum album *Hysteria*. The album purged seven singles and sold 20 million copies during the years 1987-1988. Two of the album's singles ("Armageddon It" and "Rocket") were gigantic pieces of poo, only becoming hits based on the sheer momentum of the Leppard juggernaut and the audacity of singer Joe Eliott's power-mullet. There is no reason why this song should have been filed into my memory banks - it is only mildly significant given the amount of trash that I have since consumed. Yet my brain has chosen to remember every lyric. This is the same brain that cannot hold onto the Spanish translation of "I think I am dying. I need a doctor."

The song revolves around one main hook, in the form of a poignant question: "Are you getting it?" Many, many times that question is answered, "Yes, Armageddon It." Upon first listen, you could have no idea how doomsday figured into this whole catastrophe of a hit, because this reply is sounded out phonetically like "I'm-a-getting-it." Then, around listen #2 one realizes that one is privy to some kind of sinister wordplay, a dialect that the band assuredly deemed "fucking brilliant" during the writing process.

"Armageddon It" is insipid, vulgar and trite. For this reason, I also believe it to be a shining example of America's tone in 1987. It would never have occurred to a majority of the record-buying public that lyrics like these ("Pull it. Pull it. Trigger the gun.") were any less important than books being delivered by Updike. This was the year during which the decade went off the rails, just before the population entered rehab or began to attend Pilates class. The country was deeply imbued in a collective conscious where nothing was off limits, where anything could be bought and where any problem could be dimmed by 19 rails of blow.

Injecting Def Leppard into this particular decade was masterful work on the part of our creator. The band sensed no irony in their fame. This bravado would have fallen flat in any year after 1992 but Def Leppard hit the sweet spot, dropping affable hits on a public that also accepted bands with names like Ratt, Cinderella and Poison. They've sold a panty-dropping 65 million albums. To put that into perspective, the top three albums of 2008 sold a *combined seven million copies*. These sales were bolstered by lines like "You know you got it. So don't rock it. You know you got it." It really makes you wonder about the human race, and where it was headed before thermal replaced spandex.

When The Thing is in full gear, I will sometimes role-play that I am the singer. Especially in this song, when Elliot suggests that the guitarist tear into an unusually horrific solo. I mouth along "C'mon Steve, get it!" just before he mauls the fret board with ill-advised wizardry. Unfortunately, Steve is no longer Armageddon It because he died in 1991, after downing painkillers and allegedly consuming a triple vodka, a quadruple vodka and a double brandy within 30 minutes. He will serve as an example of those who never came back from the dark side of the 80's, adjusting poorly to a life that didn't involve excess.

It is very easy to point out the absurdity of "Armageddon It" now but in the interest of full disclosure, I owned the single on both twelve inch and cassingle (an equally absurd format, with fidelity that sounded like the vocals were being played through the other side of a mattress). By the time *Hysteria* was released, I had seen Def Leppard eight times over the course of two albums. I carved their their logo into my school desk, spooged myself when I learned the first chords to "Photograph" and did not have hair dissimilar to bassist Rick Savage (note: his real last name). It is not that I am judging anyone for writing this song, nor for pumping fists along with its melodies. It's more that we were all that stupid for feeling emotion when we sang it.

"Armageddon It" became a Top 20 hit in the UK and reached #3 on the USA pop charts in 1988. Right now it is #1 with a bullet in my head, stuck in The Thing until the next jam takes over my airwaves.

woe was me

I am in a Berlin apartment, looking over at my boyfriend who I will break up with tonight, who will leave this dimwitted 'living together' experiment and who will have solid ground for telling everyone that I know that I'm impossible to deal with in the long term. Looking at him over there writing his play, I can't help but wonder why I haven't progressed emotionally from my first real relationship, one that I can't help but put on paper tonight. The tale of Dan's Diary.

I met Dan through a dial-up modem in 1996. It was a challenge to access the World Wide Web in those days, let alone view anything that loaded in under five minutes. I had just been given a monstrous laptop from my new employer, which accessorized perfectly with my lunchbox-sized cell phone. I began doing something called "surfing," which meant finding websites linked from others.

As everyone knows, the Internet was originally invented for scientists and lonely gay people. It was the shot-heard-round-the-world for men who had the brains of DNA researchers but the abs of a pastry chef. It was also the most embarrassing place to meet someone romantically, thought of as a sewer where rats met and bred. Thousands of mid-nineties relationships were given false beginnings to the outside world. "We met in a bar, mom" was much easier to swallow than "We met in an AOL message forum about Vulcan role-playing."

My modem was constantly dialing, trying to find a local number that would connect me to America Online's labyrinth of message boards. It was during one of these sessions that I discovered Dan's online diary.

It was a seemingly simple site, which required hours of programming back then. The idea that somebody would regularly document his life was crazy talk. The webmasters of those days were regarded as gurus, pulling off something that any three-year old can now do with an iPad and stolen wi-fi.

The truth is, Dan's blogging preceded the term by ten years. He was a Woe Pioneer.

I read as many entries as I could in one day, before packing my massive black laptop into my bag and flying to Cincinnati for a business trip. I finished the final entries on an airport floor, dialed up through a newfangled port on a public pay phone.

There is no understating what Dan's Diary did to me. It made me feel like there was some other young man exactly like me, a real person capable of breathing the same air that I breathed. He even liked my favorite band, a semi obscure shoe-gazing outfit called Spiritualized. It didn't seem possible there was someone on the end of another computer talking about the things that moved me, the things that ached in my head everyday, the things that I couldn't tell another person.

I wrote the email to Dan all night long. I knew that it was a futile exercise; that I would never see a reply from someone who probably received dozens of emails every day (dozens was, like, a lot back then).

The letter was the most honest thing I had ever written. It was the first true proclamation of my homo-whatever and one of the few times that I showed all of my cards. It scared me as I wrote it, thoughts that I knew I could never pull back from my fingers. I confessed my huge high school crush, unlocked images of my abusive father and quoted my favorite Mazzy Star song lyrics. I pushed send as soon as it was finished, for fear that I would lose my connection.

Then, nothing.

Then, something.

Two days later an email arrived. It was surprisingly long and began with a confession. Dan was not, in fact, writing the diary in real time. He was posting bits of his early 20's experience while now in his late 20's. It was more a memoir and less a diary. This did not bother me because he went on to write the best letter that I have ever read. It was a letter to me, it was lengthy and specifically told me that Dan had written the diary in hopes of creating a situation exactly like this. It was like a songwriter telling me that I was the guy from the lyrics in his songs.

I walked around the East Village 90 times, re-reading the dot matrix copy of his letter and trying to fathom my response. I had nobody to call because I was entirely in the closet, without a soul to talk to about the chemicals screaming through my brain. I was at the emotional level of a seventh grader, having never had feelings for the dozens of girls that I'd felt up and dumped. This was all frighteningly new.

I wrote back a letter that rivaled the length of something written by Tolstoy, unable to stop myself but sure that its length and contents would put Dan off me. My new letter, further pouring out my heart and pathetic feelings, might as well have come from the psych ward at Lennox Hill Hospital. If it were a Harry Potter howler, it would have screamed "I AM IN LOVE WITH YOU AND I DONT EVEN KNOW YOU."

Then nothing.

Then something.

Lots of something. Hundreds of pages of letters flew back and forth over the next two months, often even slowing down the progress of the website, which angered many addicts of the diary. Dan regularly received letters from bereaved men in their sixties who were tired of watching Dallas re-runs and ignoring their wives. He confessed to me that many of these men offered him money, plane tickets and promises. They felt like they knew him from the diary and were in love with him too. The thing was, my creepy love was requited.

We both changed our calling plans so that we could talk into the night. I would dial his nine digits into my plastic Connair touchtone, praying that my roommates could not hear my fluttered conversation. I would lie on my mattress like a fifteen year-old, twirling the cord between my fingers and toes.

The first call was the most terrifying thing I had ever done, besides feeling up the girls previously mentioned.

"This is weird."
"This is really weird."
"Are you breathing normally?"
"No."
"Me neither. I might have an embolism"
"Don't."
"Ok."
"What's an embolism?"

We were pushing the three-month mark when one of us finally brought up the idea of meeting. He lived in Boston and I lived in New York, so the distance was surmountable enough if we weren't so chicken shit.

Even a social retard now knows that you should move a relationship offline within a week. It was 1996 and I was not even experienced enough to ask for a picture. Keep in mind this was when a modem made a high pitched shrill upon dialup. Therapists hadn't yet established protocol for their loser clients' online fantasies.

Our relationship was exactly how I wanted it to be. Any chance that it might deflate was just too scary to consider. So, we continued until I finally had to be in Boston for work a couple more months later.

"I am going to be in Boston."
"My Boston?"
"Yeah, your Boston. The one at the end of the Mass Pike."
"Oh."

We were both witty on paper or after 2 A.M. 11 to 2 was not our strike zone.

"So, we should meet?"
"This is going to be a disaster."

"Challenger Level disaster."
"Exactly."
"We have to."
"I know."

Everything about the meeting was ill conceived, from the location to the plan. We were to meet in my room at The Park Plaza Hotel, an institution that was glorious in 1962 but, despite hanging onto its prime real estate, could never quite maintain that original polish. It was where wives went to drink champagne and men went to hammer their secretaries.

I was so nervous that I could not work out a proper first date. First, there was the ludicrous proposition that somebody should see us and learn of our homosexuality, that one of our friends would see us and report us to The Queer Department at the FBI. Or worse, out me to my friends. This is how my mind thought in the closet.

Second, I had no idea where we could go and be comfortable picking up the dozens of conversation threads of the past five months.

Third. Oh god. This was happening.

I was pacing at seven, when he was supposed to arrive. I was frantic by 7:20. By 8:00, I was nearly throwing up, imagining that he had panicked and fled for home. I pondered running through Cambridge with a boom box overhead playing "Fade Into You."

Then a knock on the door.

I had told myself that I would not look through the keyhole but I did anyway. Think about how many people have been inappropriately judged through a keyhole since its invention.

I opened the door to find the opposite of my dreams. Dan was, it seemed, human. His hair was thinning, his waist was expanding and his glasses were the size of icecaps. He looked twice as frightened as me, which put him at DEFCON Five. I invited him in.

I was so busy being nervous that I could not even process how to handle things. Physically, this was not the man of my dreams. My mind was trying to catch up, to figure out if I could accept this substitute. Had I simply expected too much? Were the pages more important than the cover?

He knew before he even came into the room. Being older and a natural fatalist, he knew that it was going to be a tragic occasion. He had driven around for an hour stalling the inevitable but eventually swallowed hard and walked forward.

There we were, alone in the room, already weary by the seconds of anxiety. I thought about the condoms I'd placed in the Bible drawer next to the bed, wondering what I'd been thinking. Neither of us could get out a full sentence.

"So what do..."
"Not sure. Do we..."
"I guess stay or..."
"Maybe something just here..."
"In the room. Movie, maybe..."

We pay-per-viewed a thriller starring Gina Davis, filmed when her career had promise and zing. We eyeballed it sitting inches apart on the full-sized bed, both pretending to watch the movie and both doing the opposite. Our minds were racing, doing triage. Neither of our diagnoses seemed promising. This silent hemorrhaging continued for over two hours, at which point Gina Davis' career began its descent.

"That was horrible."
"She'll never recover."
Dead silence.
"So, I should go. You think?"
"Yeah. I think."
"OK."

A walk to the door. A horribly confused moment. An exit.

Three days passed before we interacted again. The meeting was such a letdown that neither of us had recovered well. I came home and called in sick with what every New Yorker claims ails them (sushi food poisoning).

I didn't listen to melodramatic music. I did not write in a journal. I did not drink or smoke too much. I just wallowed on the bed in my tiny bedroom, trying to figure out how everything could be fixed. I didn't want Dan out of my life - I just wanted the memory of The Park Plaza Hotel to be wiped from my brain. I wanted to go back to the way things were when I did not know what he looked like, or that our chemistry could be so disrupted. I wanted my virtual reality.

It was never the same. Dan kept me at the center of his life, while I tried to be more absentminded about his existence. I used to crave his emails but now they plagued me. My guilt over this made me feel even worse. He called me out as I dodged him, which made me even more cagey and distant. His tone took that of a person losing love, yet I read it as that of a stalker. He became somebody who would not take "no" when it came to being in my life, clinging to the feelings we had before we'd met. I became a giant asshole.

So, it ended. I don't remember how. It may have been something quick after one of his long, confused emails. It may have been one of my brief letters with lines that were meant to be read between. Either way, I found ways to occupy The Space of Dan in my life, locking him into the part of my brain that stores confusion, a terrible quadrant filled with hallways that my father had previously walked alone.

I still think about Dan all of the time. It happens at the best times, like when I discover a new band or read a new book. Or travel somewhere that he would never want to go because they don't have hamburgers. I smirk and laugh and have a moment that nobody else could fathom. I imagine that he is there, comprehending.

Getting older frames things in ways that they were not intended to be hung. The time between Dan's Diary and now has knocked down the bad things and brightened the good ones. I can only remember how romantic it all was and am sure that I will never feel this way again, mostly because my innocence is now polluted to the point of toxicity.

I will feel this strongly about someone else, someday. But I worry that the marker has been set too high, if anything can ever achieve the intensity of Dan.

It's strange how two hours in a hotel room can completely fuck with your whole life.

florence defaced by graffiti, declared ugly and depressing

In what seems like less than a decade, Firenze's famous beauty and charm has gone directly into the crapper.

The city has never been particularly effective at fighting miscreant ink but now it's turned into a real doghouse. The markings are everywhere, even at eye level on the walls around the Duomo. Alleyways and small streets are tagged dozens of times. Many large, wooden doors are blasted with paint. Signs are hardest hit, rendering bus schedules useless at many stops.

It seems like a great time to be a police officer in Florence. There are endless amounts of tourist photos to be taken, plenty of text messages to be written and bottomless espressos to be sipped from tiny paper cups.

Cops in the city center socialize in circles, looking as if they might break out a hacky sack at any moment. Bus and train station rent-a-cops seem to come standard with headphones and MP3 players. They all love to whistle.

Perhaps the police's apathy makes the Taggers work harder for attention. The words don't support this theory though. They are banal tags, mostly names and initials. There is no hint of artistic aspiration, like with the murals of Santiago or the clever Banksys that turn up in

London. One can only picture 15 year-old nimrods doing what 15 year-old nimrods do - defacing and then running.

The lack of purpose involved in all of this is frustrating and makes the streets look like the set of a bad 1980's rap video. There's no "fuck the police" or political statement, no reason given for the defacement of centuries-old buildings. It's just a bunch of crap spray painted on a wall.

One person seems obsessed with tagging the word "yogurt" as many as ten times in a five-block radius of The Uffizi. Another person has taken to simply dumping buckets of paints on ATM's.

There is probably much that I don't know about the war on graffiti here. Perhaps police squads roam the streets at night. Or perhaps a special commission has already been called.

Maybe the mayor isn't taking three-hour lunches as I imagine in my head, and instead sits in his office, pining over how his city is being devalued. Maybe the tourism commission, whose Information Points are even tagged up, are not operating with blinders on.

Maybe there's a master plan in the works to make Florence beautiful again, to make it look less like the inside of a toilet stall. Or maybe we all need just a little bit more yogurt and don't know it.

star trek in french, as told by somebody who doesn't speak french

Tonight I watched Star Trek in Cahors, France. I was the only person in the theatre during the 18:30 showing. 18:30 means 6:30pm. The film was overdubbed. I do not speak French. Here is my summation of the plot of this fine film:

A big, squidlike clam ship tries to eat another ship that looks like the one at the beginning of the old TV episodes, except it's groovier and more J.J. Abrams-looking. A very mean man (with tribal face tattoos that look like they were designed at a shop called Damage Ink) seems to be behind the whole thing.

The Star Trek ship crashes into the mean ship, but not before the captain sends his pregnant wife off on a smaller ship. She gives birth within sixty seconds in that movie way and they name him via speakerphone. They call him Jeem.

We are introduced to a boy called Spuck. He is being schooled in logic and bunch of numbers that I can't count to in French. Wynona Ryder, in her much ballyhooed return, gives him a talking to. She seems like she always seems in movies: like Wynona Ryder with a costume on.

We learn that Jeem is now a grown up playa with the ladies. He channels a young W and rampages through some cocktails. His hair looks died orange-brown. He meets a girl and they discuss ducks or something, depending on if you trust my translation. A fight ensues during which Jeem decides to grow up. People begin calling him Keerk.

It should be mentioned that characters are yelling at each other in French a lot.

Jeem bangs some green lady.

There is some mishagas in a room with a lot of people. Everyone is assigned to ships. Keerk is given to The Enterprise and boards the ship. I figure out who Sulu is based on his ethnicity. Bones is obviously Bones. Chekhov is by far the hottest and demands my attention.

Keerk and Spuck are cross with each other, in front of their captain. Spuck has razor burn. Somehow, suddenly, The Enterprise does battle with the clam ship. Mean Tattoo Man is up to something involving blood or DNA or big needles. We learn that Tattoo Man is something called a Voolcan.

The second reel clicks through and I am more confused than a circus clown performing an abortion. Everyone seems to be shouting numbers as Keerk parachutes into a Voolcan outpost, then fights with more Tattoo Men. Sulu shows up in a hot-shit silver number and does Kill Bill battle with the dudes, too.

They succeed in doing something but then something bad happens. Spuck acts logically and many people yell into their wrists. Hot Checkhov saves Keerk and Sulu, who then beam back onto the ship while spooning.

Tattoo Man has captured the old captain and tortures him with holograms of beautiful women, then feeds him a weird scorpion. It is at this point that I realize that no person remaining on the ship seems to be older than 20 years old. Spuck has kicked his razor burn and does the Voolcan pinch on Keerk. The audience claps.

Keerk ends up on a planet of ice with bad CGI monsters attacking him. An older Spuck saves him. A series of flashbacks confuses the English Speaking Audience. There might be something about a time portal. Nothing else makes sense and I start having rude thoughts about Checkhov until this sequence is over.

Keerk and Old Spuck enter some kind of weird warehouse with some character who wears a bomber jacket and appears to be somebody named Scutty. Everyone gets cross with each other. Old Spuck takes off and does the "Live Long and Prosper" thing, which I only understand because of the finger action.

Keerk and Scutty get beamed back to the present day Enterprise. Scotty gets pumped through something that looks like a Habitrail.

Reel three kicks in as Keerk and Spuck become cross with each other again. Shit goes down, Spuck leaves the bridge in a huff and Keerk becomes captain. Spuck comes back to the bridge and makes up with Keerk. They come close to kissing.

Some kind of plan is devised.

Spuck and Keerk beam into Tattoo Man's lair. He is not chuffed and everyone becomes cross with each other. Spuck ends up leaving on some ship but only by calling Keerk by his first name, Jeem. They almost kiss again.

Keerk fights Tattoo Man on a set that is about the tenth homage to Jedi. Spuck breaks some necklace-in-the-sky thing with his ship. This pisses off Tattoo Man, who seems to be everywhere at once. Keerk shoots Tattoo Man's henchman in the nuts and sends him into space.

Keerk rescues the old captain, who didn't die from the scorpion-thing or the holograms. Spuck, Keerk and Captain are beamed safely back to The Enterprise. A final battle with Tattoo Man and his clam ship ensues and the bad guys are sent into the portal from the other part that I didn't understand.

The Enterprise almost gets pulled apart but it doesn't. Everyone seems relieved. Back on land, Spuck meets his older self and gets a talking to. The word "logic" is bandied about. Spuck nearly tongue-kisses older Spuck.

Keerk gets a medal and looks smug. The crew gets a curtain call on the deck of The Enterprise, in a kind of a gay Broadway way. A sequel is assured.

The End.

whilst traveling via eurail

Gare Austerlitz

Paris Austerlitz Station at dawn. A security guy roams the building on a Segway, thus stripping himself of any authority.

The coffee shop contains one employee breaking open bags of filters, her face giving away the disbelief that she's pulled this crappy shift. Two late-teen looking girls clutch their bags with a remember-what-dad-said look. The board is lit up with departures but no gate numbers. The hall is train-less.

This is the best time to travel. Back at home, I have a terrifically difficult time pulling myself out of bed before ten. Out here I book morning trains and force myself out of bed. The jump from the top bunk always marks the moment I am asleep (up there) and the moment I am awake (when my gross motor skills jar to life, in an attempt to save my life as my feet hit the cold floor.)

A conductor is whistling, destroying the quiet vibe of the big, hollow room. The clock strikes six. I yawn and everyone follows suit. The whole thing is more of a mingle than it is a morning rush. I count ten people eating croissants. I am definitely in France.

Paris to Cahors

I board the train, pushing a button that opens the doors with a wheeze. I will push through Chateauroux, Limoges and Brive, at which point I will switch to a second train. Five hours, door to door.

You could not have paid me to fly. I'm a Theroux-ist, falling for these big beasts that rock and sway and creak and arrive where you want to go, not thirty miles away at a deceivingly-named airport. Every promise about plane travel has become a lie, with the exception of the time you make up in the air. The day that I pay extra in an exit row is the day that I invent a time machine and be done with it.

The Eurail Pass made things simple for me. I had imagined agents rolling their eyes at my mangled French and instead got a lightning-fast transaction, my booking complete in seconds. The train was rather gorgeous and "stoked me out," as my friend Brian likes to say. I fell back into my chair and basked in front of a tray table that was big enough to simultaneously hold my coffee and laptop, which is all that I want out of life.

We rode through misty fields. Little houses with chimneys and men who looked like Girard Depardieu. Enough goldenrod to make anyone reach for a Zyrtec. Castles that looked too fake to be real. I fell asleep and dreamed about being at the bottom of a well.

Toulouse to Girona

Another station. Rap plays through the speaker of a teenager's phone. It sounds tinny and I lament the death of fidelity. The artist raps in French and mimics American hip-hop, sounding just as big a clown as ours do. He wants money. He want cars. He wants fame. He demands it. What a goddamned bore.

At the counter. I hand her my Eurail pass and try my French. She laughs and makes my booking in English, trying to teach me how to say things in French at the same time. She shows me how to talk with phlegm in my syllables. She is more than a booking agent. She is my savior.

I get on the train and listen to Husker Du really loud and consider losing ten pounds. Then order a croissant from the trolley.

Girona to Parpignon

I'm on board the SCNF, which is wonderful and punctual. I sit across from an elderly couple. The man yells as he talks and the woman hushes him after every fourth word. I don't need to speak French to know that they've been together for years and years. She smiles as she shushes, looking at her man in a way that suggests the kind of toleration that comes with adoration.

The train is magnificent, a real sleek beauty that doesn't befit my CBGB's t-shirt. Ruby carpets and black, pinstriped seats. It pulls out exactly on time, rolling past the graffiti that accompanies just about any stretch with concrete walls. Much like the French rappers, any retard with spray paint seems to tag nowadays. I strain to see some genuine art and come up short. Just lots of names and initials and wasted paint.

Parpignon to Montpelier

They are next to me, talking nonstop. Three American girls.

"Like. Like. They like. Ugh. Seriously." The poor dear can't even get three words out. "Like, I know Greg. I mean, I KNOW him, you know? Seriously." I catch the rhythms of their inflection, a sing-songy bastardization of English.

"I am sitting in traffic" (up) "and there is this guy behind me" (up) " and he is like freaking me out." (down) "Like, have you ever just been creeped out by someone for like, no reason?" (up) "Seriously" (down).

I have the backwards seat, the solo one that pits my knees against the opposing traveler's shins. They are two sleepy girls wearing airline sleepmasks. I can only hope that their eyes are closed by behind the masks, because their mouths are puppy-like and drooling. Their bags lay unattended, passports out in the open. Somewhere, their mothers are worrying, and not needlessly. Their daughters are idiots.

The train is a Talgo. It smells like the sawdust and ammonia that is used to clean the Tilt-a-Whirl after somebody spews a funnel cake.

The American girls don't stop talking for three hours. They're from a reality show generation. More talking means more screen time. "Dave Matthews. I like, can't even put him into words." The earphones are in her ears, the music playing as she talks.

I am certain that they are what keeps me from returning to America. I tell myself that it wasn't the sinkhole that had become my life. It was these girls. It was their fault.

the best hostel in france (is going off tonight)

The guy in the TKA shirt lands his beer pong toss ("Take that mother...") as the girl with curly hair is tongue-jamming her conquest, an Aussi guy who told me earlier that he was "gonna get that, mate." A nineteen year old Canadian boy sits at the bar, downing shots of bottom-shelf rum.

He's trying to keep up with the goopy-eyed girl from Portland who seems unable to discuss anything other than her boyfriend ("He totally lets me put eyeshadow on him.") Somebody drops a glass. A pregnant pause. Then the whole place whoops as the party shifts into fifth gear.

The Villa Saint Exupery in Nice, France – recognized worldwide as classy dorm digs – is filled tonight with the same energy you'd feel at a Megadeth concert. This "relaxing" and "extraordinary" place is jammed with howling patrons who have a seemingly common purpose – to create utter chaos.

It's a real pity for the owners, who would probably be happier to have a clientele of calm, snifter-whiffing women in their thirties. There's nothing that can disqualify soothing adjectives faster than a backpacker on the drink.

Still, there's good reason that the hostel is sold out tonight. It does everything right. The staff is abundant, easily handling the 100+ residents in this converted monastery. They dole out maps and directions with less disdain than I've ever witnessed, answering the most routine questions with genuine smiles. Two shuttle vans make nonstop runs to town and the airport. Laundry is washed and folded for five Euros. Vending machines sell anything that you could have forgotten back home, from shaving cream to condoms (mate).

A big, stainless steel kitchen gives plenty of room to move but few people make their own meals because the in-house chef is just so damned good. On one occasion I was served roast veal with rosemary potatoes, ratatouille and green beans. The next night was some salmon concoction that looked straight out of a good episode of *Top Chef*. I caressed every piece of food with my fork before I ate it, just to make sure it was real and not some kind of too-long-on-the-road mirage.

The Chapel is the hostel's star attraction. A massive room wrapped in a stained glass wall, it also features a balcony full of free, high-speed-charged computers. Strewn about are couches, a tuned grand piano and a wide-screen television. Outside of The Chapel are three sitting areas, one complete with a fireplace.

The bar is, as mentioned, quite alive. House beer and wine only relieve patrons of one Euro and late-night drinkers can always grab a brewskie from the vending machine. Plates of brick-sized brownies are also available at the bar, scarfed down as fast as they can be made. It's the kind of room that is impossible to be lonely in.

The dorm rooms are a bit cramped, holding as many as 13 beds. The designers realized that they weren't going to win any prizes with the room space afforded to them, so they wisely opted to make the common areas so attractive that nobody would bother with the beds, other than to sleep. Any complaints about the dorm rooms would seem common for most hostels – more showers, toilet paper and less inexperienced drinkers.

The Villa Saint Exupery's only downfall might not be its own doing. Reviews and articles about the hostel are so glowing that many people booking might not take into account that this is, after all, a playpen for backpackers. It doesn't matter how big the beds are – they're still littered with empty peanut butter jars and Stephanie Meyer books.

The reviews give Saint Exupery a grand air – which it has in many ways – but no matter how you dress a hostel up, there's still going to be the Australian dude slapping me on the back, talking about how he'll get the girl who smells like Garnier Fructis.

A hostel is, still, just a hostel.

notes from the grand del mar hotel, san diego

Friday, 2:59pm

I am in my room, squealing like a two year-old who's been given a Mickey Mouse ice cream, the kind with chocolate ears.

I am rolling in the layers of white bedding. I now understand why dogs do that nose–to-the-grass thing in the fields of big parks. Before it seemed so queer.

I open and shut drawers and doors of thick, beautiful wood. I turn on anything electrical, from the bathtub television to the iPod speaker set that, yes, can be brought right into the crapper. I thumb every piece of linen, then Google their Italian makers' name.

Ooh la la.

The Grand Del Mar has given me this room for two nights in order to write about it. This is my first writer 'spiff' ever and I pondered not taking it for a little while, remembering all of the debate last year about accepting free things and the fury of righteousness and vitriol that followed. I have decided to join Club Spiff because I have realized that I am not a journalist and that I'm a writer. A writer will write about anything that inspires and for me, right now, it's an ottoman the size of The Ottoman.

The doorbell rings. A princely bellhop delivers a plate of fresh fruit. I contemplate telling him that I'm a frog in need of a kiss to complete this fairy tale, but instead usher him out before I say something even more embarrassing.

"I love you," I whisper as he closes the door.

Friday, 11:11pm

I have had wine.

I could eat this. I could chew it and swallow it and regurgitate it and eat it again. The winding halls that feel like a castle, the mismatched wooden furniture that somehow matches, the carpeted walkway to my room that feels perfect on my non-flip-flopped feet.

Over the two days I will steal seven bars of perfectly crafted soap. I will place two in an inner compartment of my luggage each morning, only to return several hours later with new bars in their place. I will wonder if there is a Soap Fairy, a milk-white soul who places fresh bars without any judgment because she knows at home I'm currently working with three-fers from the $.99 store.

It is not the five-star treatment or the real leather that does me in. I feel this exact same way when the generator spurts out on a remote island, causing the goat to actually stop goating because the silence shocks even the animal (goat=WTF).

It's not even the chocolate-covered Oreo on the pillow. The point is that they didn't just foil-wrap a regular chocolate and have instead mainlined into my dessert fantasies. I feel the same love in this strange, massive hotel as I do when an islander proudly shows me the straw cushions that function like a box spring and says, "Nice, you see?"

Except tonight, admittedly, I have Skinemax and a nipper of Jameson's.

Saturday, 12:20pm

I turn up to my first-ever golf lesson wearing jeans and a track jacket. One wink and a swift golf cart ride back to my room later, I return wearing a collared shirt and khakis. Clearly I've never golfed before – my upbringing leaned much more towards free government cheese than it did trust fund clubhouses.

My pro is a guy named Wyatt and he feels like the kind of person who could teach me anything. His approach is laced with positive reinforcement. By the end of the lesson I want him to travel through time and adopt me in 1974, the year that I accidentally dropped the thing on the ground and learned that my biological father could become The Other Kind of Dad.

Wyatt is of the "divots are good" school and encourages me to rip up as much perfectly manicured lawn as possible. I excel at destroying the turf and am given a huge pat on the back at every swing. "Whoa Tom. That's great! Not on the mark but your form is great!"

I think again and again of my father and learning how to hit a baseball and riding a bike and fishing and hunting. How my bowels turned inside out at the thought of any lesson he'd ever given me, because it would always turn into a tirade and eventually The Belt. "This is how you learn then."

Then Wyatt. Chuckling at my failures, yet raising my shoulder a tweak before my swing, a "Better!" after I drive the ball into a hopeless, westward tizzy. He offers a stance suggestion that helps my ball miraculously fly in a straight-ish direction. "Better!" Then he shows me how to twist my fingers and I execute a strong shot, straight up the fairway, like the guys on TV. "Oh man! That's gorgeous. Exactly how to do it."

Wyatt drives me back to the pro shop on the silly little golf cart. He is the best teacher I have ever had. I will never see him again.

Saturday, 4:44pm

The Renaissance Massage. You cannot know.

Step One: Coat guest in mud ("from Germany") and place them in a pod that is not dissimilar to those in *Alien, Avatar, Battlestar Galactica,* etc. Push the button and gently submerge the guest in a free floating bath, an experience that feels like something between being a fetus and living inside a waterbed mattress. Witness guest panic for thirty seconds, then watch them have the most serene 30 minutes of his life.

Step Two: Let the guest shower off the mud in a room with thirteen nozzles pointing from the ceiling and three walls, and not in a "hose him down" prison intake way. Make sure to turn all nozzles on before guest enters because guest will take three to seven minutes to figure it out on his own.

Step Three: Give the guest a 60 minute massage in such a way that his thoughts go to a Hawking Place, no matter whether he graduated state college with a 2.7 or not (but only because of the one semester where he got a 1.6 because he fell in with the wrong crowd).

Watch guest walk straight into the door frame upon exiting the room, because guest has lost perception of reality.

Saturday, 11:33pm

I spend the last night having a dinner that food writers would call "scrumptious," "succulent" and "mouth-watering." It's as simple as pulling my body from my room to Amaya, the hotel's fancy-schmancy restaurant, where I order unfiltered merlot and beef. And a sensible salad.

I spend the meal much less focused on the food than on the staff outside. There is a wedding on the big lawn and there are dozens of waiters floating around. It's a quiet algorithm playing itself out, all of these waiters whisking off to fetch more glasses, just before plating duck or turning up with a new napkin.

I want to talk to the people who work here, to give them a few drinks and ask them to spill their guts. Are they really as happy as they look? I have a feeling that they are.

I return to my own dinner and realize that my wine glass has been refilled, even though I'd been ordering by the glass. The waiter comes by and winks, then whispers, "It was half-full. Somebody's got to finish the bottle."

I think maybe everyone who works here is a glass half-full kind of person. I think maybe this is why I love certain places over others. Straw or pillow-top, it comes down to the spirit of the people who run venues where other people lay their heads. The better ones know that the care can't be faked, that every person inherently knows a put-on, and that we appreciate the real thing more than wine or chocolate.

Ain't it the truth.

the patron saint of my round-the-world trip

May 20, 2001, Logan Airport, Boston

I have blagged my way into the British Airways lounge by complimenting the check-in lady on her silver dollar-sized earrings. They're hideous.

First Class lounges often find me buzzed on queer combinations of cheese, water crackers, Kahlua, Campari and any other kind of odd liquor/liqueur that it never strikes me to try at home. Today is no exception.

The guy across from me is wearing a cardigan and reading *Yacht World*. I want to put him in front of a speaker and blare Ramones and shake him from his necktie existence, to give him a tour of a world where he doesn't have to gingerly cross one leg over the other. He's fine wine and I'm a Jello shot. He can have his yacht and I'll keep Joey & Dee Dee & Johnny & Tommy.

I cherish these odd shaped rooms, full of stained chairs and stinky-pitted businessmen. They portray an excellence that is the opposite of the double-coupon clipping class from which I am bred. Here I am regal because I can eat cubes of Monterrey Jack for free.

May 22, 2011, Hotel JL No. 76, Amsterdam

It's been a longstanding dream of mine to be the first person to sleep in a new hotel room. I'm checking that one off tonight at this hotel, which is in previews.

The room is a monster success – sleek, big, and comfortable. A flat-screen-TV-in-the-shower kind of joint. There is zero aroma of cleaning products and only a slight waft of fresh paint.

I become obsessed with taking the room's virginity, making sure to try everything for the first time. I open curtains, drawers, cabinets, the mini bar and sewing kits. I am the first one to go potty in this room, and the first to realize that the bathroom has no windows.

I imagine the things that will happen in here. Children will be conceived. Someone will cry in bed after hearing bad news from home. A woman will say "aw, fuck" in the bathroom as she realizes that she's forgotten Playtex. Another will pace as she waits to find out if the pregnancy test reads positive, contemplating abortion.

A couple will have an hour of silence as they each imagine the words that will hurt their partner the most, then turn those thoughts into perfectly formed, actualized syllables. Relationships will end. Relationships will begin. A teenager will suffer through having to share a room with his parents. A drunken man will punch a mirror and require stitches.

Someone will smoke way too much weed and have three traumatic hours on the bed. A man will dance to James Brown in his underwear. A woman will try on four outfits, only to leave in the first one. A man will be impotent on his wedding night.

And surely, someone will die.

May 25, 2011, Deli Italy Restaurant, Paris

The restaurant tic. I have to find the right restaurant. The right one is the one that is stumbled upon, gut feeling, after a lot of wandering.

They all call to me like hookers:

"I'm cute."
Too tarty.

"I'm adventurous."
I was looking for vanilla.

"I'm the unknown secret."
You know you're working with two-week old scallops.

There it is. Italian place, rammed to the rafters with chalkboard specials. 20 tables, if that. Put me in the corner. I am in Le Marais and I want to get wine-drunk and stare at gossipy French homosexuals.

I order a lifeboat of antipasto, which comes piled on a cutting board, all kinds of pretty. A marvel. Prosciutto and eggplant and mozzarella and artichokes and mushrooms. Some other kind of pig, too. I consume it like an aristocrat for the first minute, then like a caveman for the next nine.

50cl of Tellus rouge fuels the operation and stains my left cuff. I don't know what a cl is. It's a lot.

I am people-watching as the spaghetti Bolognese arrives via a dumbwaiter above the bar. It is fresh and is as sweet as Bambi. It is gone as fast as it arrived. I'll come back here every time I'm in Paris.

The queens continue to gossip as I leave. "*Regardez le départ homosexuelle Américaine. Il est gros.*" Yeah, yeah, yeah.

May 30th, Pelikan Restaurant, Stockholm

I have wanted to meet Lola Akinmade for over two years. She is the Spirit of *Matador*, blasting positivity through the staff, readers and students. You've probably seen her somewhere on the site, jumping in a photo. It's her thing.

Lola does not know that she was the patron saint of my 2009 round-the-world. I felt her on my shoulder, pushing me forward and somehow protecting me. I am not at all religious but it was a religious kind of feeling. It was something else to have this person who feels so pure-but-not-puritanical keeping an eye on you.

That's what tenses my guts as I go to meet her. Given my impression of Lola – the pure thing – I wonder how in the world she'd even give me the time of day. My writing is turgid and weird and filled with the kind of things that make therapists drool. How's *Matador*'s soul guru going to hang with the guy who sucks face with randoms in Chilean tree houses?

Then she's there with a huge hug and a second one for good measure. Genuine hugs. The biggest smile you'll ever see. Like she'd been waiting forever to meet me. Like I'd been waiting forever to meet her. Fear deflated and happiness elated.

Her newish husband and stunning sister joined us for a traditional Swedish meal, which did include meatballs. I tried to keep up with Lola's unique accent; a little Nigerian, a little DC and a little Swedish.

We talked about things that travel writers do. Places, things in places, people in places and inspiration. Not to lick the balls of *Matador*, but we also talked about what an incredible ride it's been for the site, and the people that it has brought up with it. Lola's been here for a while and can step back and see lives changing.

I reminisced about how I had never written anything before *Matador*. Two blogs later and I was on a conference call with Ross Borden and David Miller, both of whom talk like a cross between The Dalai Lama and Ton Loc.

"Tom, it would be so boss if you edited our Life section. We totally feel your aura of blues and reds and whatnot. Straight up, we like your shit." I didn't have any experience or training or regard for how long sentences run on, nor did I have any training in maintaining a website. I had, and still have, a fierce disdain for coding. "Yes, but you have heart, and that is all you need in this world. The world is like one crazy ride on a unicorn, but don't get distracted by the horn. We have a dope feeling, dawg. Get some shit done motherfucker!" Hired.

I think about those in *Matador*U and wonder if they really get it. I have both feet back in music business now and see it with musicians all of the time – there's luck, but if you're really good then you'll get your shot. You just have to find the outlet. *Matador* is one of the few places that allows for the travel writing shot, and the encouragement when you still kind of suck. It's an important platform if you're a jumper.

There are so many quirks about The *Matador* Approach To Publishing that I love that are a part of me. To illustrate what's behind the curtain, I'm looking back at my old emails and a David Miller email to the staff on September 28, 2009 will serve as an example:

Reading back through this I found the words "dizzying selection," as in: Belgium produces a dizzying selection of 600 beers, including Haacht's new fruit beer.

Oh no.

There was also this: "luxuriant decadence" as in: Marx and Engels wrote their Communist Manifesto here, perhaps provoked by the luxuriant decadence of chocolate.

Shit.

Ladies and gentleman, I'm hereby declaring war on anything that sounds like canned writing. If a single platitude comes up in a draft, please delete it immediately, and if it seems like you're deleting every other word– "polishing a turd" as carpenters like to say–then let's question publishing it at all.

For a year and a half I winged it. Or wung it. Where's my editor? My most frequent commenter, other than Tim Patterson and Julie Schwietert, was Lola. The more whacked out my stories would get, the more she'd encourage me. She'd find the pieces of my writing that I was most afraid to type and zero in on them, pointing out those exact things as positives in the comments.

I realize that Lola effuses positivity in a way that is not put on, which is to be savored. But I think I'm getting something more now, as I talk to her here in Stockholm. I think I'm realizing that Lola would only plug herself into a job where there is love. And care. And compassion. And spirit. She'd never spend a day working for a boss who screams. Any guidebook or travel outlet would die to have her but she has instincts about what will make her fulfilled.

She's found that in *Matador*. She doesn't care that *Matador* is held together by duct tape and wi-fi. She does it because she feels connected with whatever energy comes out of our ragtag group. That's the purity that guided me.

I get it now. Her divinity is just simply love.

notes from a round-the-world comedown

I'M NOT MUCH FOR handholding. Or extended hugging. Or for feeling vulnerable. Ask the exes. They'll tell you what caused them to kick me to the curb – my ridiculous independence and need to hold onto it, even in moments when I'm not supposed to be holding it all together.

This moment, though, finds me somewhere on the border of drama and melodrama. It's a state of being that I can only call 'away-sickness,' a term I've adopted for when I feel the pull to leave home and can't. Most people want their own down comforter and indoor plumbing – I crave a straw bed and a boxed hole in the ground.

I moved to Los Angeles three months ago, following a year of worldwide wandering, during which I lived in twelve countries over twelve months. The idea of the trip was to embrace the concept of slow travel – going places and then planting my fanny for thirty days. What I didn't expect is that this would leave me homesick for twelve countries, all of which adapted and adopted me.

The cracks showed themselves in February, when I purchased a 44-ounce bottle of Heinz Ketchup. I looked down and realized that this wasn't a pit stop on my trip, that I was buying at least 50 burgers worth of red stuff, and that even my disgusting eating habits couldn't substantiate that much condiment craving for less than three months. I now lived here.

I tried to fill the hole. I went on $14 trips to the salad bar at Whole Foods. I decided that I 'needed' to play Ghostbusters on an Xbox and lost a dozen hours attempting to annihilate the Stay-Puff Marshmallow Man. While drinking.

I made out with guys I hardly knew. I played dumb Snow Patrol songs that made me feel weak. I went emo on an Oprah level, buying a big cork board and hanging reminders of my trip – a punched train ticket, a pack of dice from a German toy store, the Metallica ticket from Argentina, my Lothian bus pass from Edinburgh with me looking skinny in the picture because I made them take it three times.

I hit post-travel bottom after getting close and personal with a bottle of Malbec, doing what everyone does after downing a whole bottle of red. I posted a pitiful song lyric on Facebook.

Immediately a traveler friend called me. He knew what a twit I was being and wanted to spare me of my cached woe.

"What's the matter?"
"I can't explain."
"It's OK. You won't ever be able to. Just stop posting stupid shit. You look like an idiot."
"OK."

We started talking about how much I hated a rooster that hid under my hut in Malaysia, and how most mornings I wanted it dead in time for breakfast, on account of its need to begin cock-a-doodling just after I'd entered a perfectly buzzed sleep (you can get bootleg beer even in Taman Negara Park if you know the right people). I was trying to figure out how I'd become so nostalgic about something that bothered me so much at the time, and why it was something so inane that I kept coming back to.

Other things were flushed from my brain. Like Neri, a student from a small town in Italy, who was assigned to my ESL classroom for month of "camp" that even the stupidest student realized was actually school that involved monotonous songs and construction paper. To say that Neri tortured me would be an understatement – spitballs from straws, soccer balls tossed across the classroom and tantrums about any kind of accountability for these things.

His grandfather came to the school after the woman running the program finally realized that I couldn't control this pinball child. The grandfather's answer was swift and simple. He beat the tar out of the boy in the school courtyard while we all watched. The next morning Neri showed up with translated English Sharpied on his palm and offered a dutiful apology with tears and sincerity. One day later, he was flipping over desks and dumping paint on the ground.

I am sure Neri is being smacked in the head right now for some poor behavior and that he has come to expect this treatment. I think about what would have happened if I had stayed in the small town in Tuscany. Could I have broken the cycle? Did I abandon a cause that was supposed to be one of my life's biggest challenges? Or is this child simply an asshole?

And now I'm here, in the perfectly painted room with the washing machine humming, the pool outside, lit with underwater lamps and the smell of flawlessly maintained flowers making my apartment smell flowery.

Last weekend my boss conned me into going to a workshop about how to connect with 'kindred spirits' and build community. I didn't feel like they were my lot and I couldn't figure out why. It hit me on the second day. My kindred spirits are travelers.

It scares the hell out of me that I don't know how to connect with people unless I'm at a guesthouse in Laos or climbing a mountain in Chile. I don't know why making a thrifty dinner with three new friends in Queenstown is more exciting than sitting down at a fancy restaurant in Beverly Hills. I don't know why I need to meet people that I'll never see again and why the time I spend with them is more powerful than many of my lifelong relationships.

Last night I tried not to look at the photos from my trip. I hadn't given them a solid look since I've been back. But like anything, the more I told myself not to, the more I needed to see them. If you're a traveler, you get this. They made me feel everything at once. I felt sad, thrilled, joyous, festive, embarrassed, empowered, weak, lonely, powerful, doomed and unstoppable.

One other thing I keep coming back to is a Talking Heads song. One minute and fifty-one seconds into "Once In A Lifetime," David Byrne declares that there is water at the bottom of the ocean. Just like that. "There is water at the bottom of the ocean."

I keep thinking about how last year I found out that there is, indeed, water at the bottom of the ocean, and that you need only travel to find it. It's one thing to logically process that there are amazing things in amazing places. It's another to gape at them from two yards away.

This is the high I will chase as long as I live. I will do my best to remain in light.

please note

Many of the stories in this book have previously posted on Matador Network, a travel site that helped me make my way around the world. Visit them at www.matadornetwork.com A huge THANK YOU to everyone who has worked there, past and present, including Ross Borden, David Miller, Julie Schwietert Collazo, Tim Patterson, Kate Sedgwick, Lola Akinmade, Paul "Mancook" Sullivan, Ian MacKenzie, Hal Amen, Carlo Alcos, Christine Garvin, Juliane Huang, Andy Hayes and Candice Walsh.

I'd like to give special thanks to Deborah Gilbert, who edited these stories with expertise and compassion. She also pointed out that I appear to be obsessed with the words "swift" and "waft." I'd also like to thank Kate Sedgwick, who read this over with a careful eye. She is always my partner in crime, and probably my tough little sister in writing. I met her as randomly as can happen on the road and I am glad for it.

Thanks to my illustrator, Sam Means, who gets all embarrassed when people tell him that he's talented. Hey Sam – you're talented.

Thanks also to Ken Howard, who coaxed this book out of me.

Please visit my website: www.theworldisgettingsmaller.com

about the author

Tom Gates is a writer based in Los Angeles. Crispy-fried after working with some of the biggest names in the music business over fifteen years, he decided to take his head out of the guillotine and see the world, chucking a job in the process. Don't you dare call it a midlife crisis.

Several travel articles later, it became apparent to others that he was actually good at writing, even if he felt inferior and refused to use key travel writing words like "succulent," "must-see" or "mouth-watering."

He is the kid who always got a "B" instead of an "A" because his papers were 5 pages shorter than the required amount, even if they were fucking great, and he still resents several teachers whose names or faces he can't remember. He needs therapy.

Tom loves to go far, far away whenever possible. He is also pretending to be a third person right now and is obviously writing his own bio. He knows that you knew that, despite the deft maneuvering of pronouns.

Made in the USA
Lexington, KY
03 December 2014